TENN YEARS

Tennessee Williams on Stage

Books by David Kaplan

Tenn Years: Tennessee Williams on Stage (2016)

Shakespeare, Shamans, and Show Biz: An Impolite Guide to Theater History, Volume I (2013)

Tenn at One Hundred: The Reputation of Tennessee Williams (2011)

Tennessee Williams in Provincetown (2007)

Five Approaches to Acting Series (2001, 2007)

TENN YEARS

Tennessee Williams on Stage

Essays by

David Kaplan

Introduction by Thomas Keith

HANSEN PUBLISHING GROUP, LLC

Tenn Years: Tennessee Williams on Stage
Copyright © 2016 by David Kaplan and the Provincetown Tennessee Williams Theatre Festival
Introduction Copyright © 2016 Thomas Keith

22 21 20 19 18 17 16   1 2 3 4 5 6

All rights reserved. Except for brief passages quoted in newspaper, magazine, radio or television reviews, no part of this book may be reproduced in any form or by any means, electronic or mechanical, including photocopying or recording, or by an information storage and retrieval system, without permission in writing from the publisher.

ISBN: 978-1-60182-426-4 (paperback)
        978-1-60182-427-1 (ebook)

Book and book cover design by Jon Hansen

Cover photo by Antonis Achilleos, Antonis Achilleos Photography

Earlier versions of some of these essays appeared in the annual catalogs of the Provincetown Tennessee Williams Theater Festival: "The Healing Power of Love" (2008), "The Fight for Life" (2009), "Under the Influence" (2010), "Double Exposures" (2011), "The Paradise Across the Alley" (2012), "Fifty Percent Illusion" (2013), "Circle of Friends" (2014). Earlier versions of some of the occasional essays were first published as "One Arm in South Africa," *Out Africa Magazine* 20 (2014); "The Day on Which a Man Dies: Reading the Red in Tennessee Williams," *Provincetown Magazine* (2009); "The Milk Train Doesn't Stop Here Anymore: Look at What We Got Away With," *The Cape Times* (4 October 2013); "Kingdom of Earth: From Cape Town to Cape Cod and Back," *Provincetown Magazine* (2013).

Fair use quotations of published material by Tennessee Williams are from the New Directions editions of his plays, poems, and prose. www.ndpublishing.com

Hansen Publishing Group, LLC
302 Ryders Lane,
East Brunswick, NJ 08816

http://hansenpublishing.com

Dedicated to Jennifer Amengual

Contents

Acknowledgments viii
Introduction: The Talent that Survives x

The Annual Festival Essays

Tennessee Williams in Provincetown (2006) 2
The Late Late Show (2007) 8
The Healing Power of Love (2008) 20
The Fight for Life (2009) 26
Under the Influence (2010) 38
Double Exposures (2011) 52
The Paradise Across the Alley: Tennessee Williams and Music (2012) 62
Chorus Girls Photographic Essay 72
Fifty Percent Illusion: Tennessee Williams and Women (2013) 78
Circle of Friends (2014) 88
Tenn Years: Tennessee Williams in Provincetown, 2006–2015 100

Occassional Essays

Hotel Plays Photographic Essay 116
The Hotel Plays 122
One Arm in South Africa: "Stirring Up Feelings Without Feeling Nothing" Myself 134

The Day On Which A Man Dies: Reading the Red in Tennessee Williams 140

The Milk Train Doesn't Stop Here Anymore: Look at What We Got Away With..150

Kingdom of Earth: From Cape Town to Cape Cod and Back..154

The Two-Character Play and Matisse 162

Nineteen Eighty: Surviving Beyond What is Acceptable 168

Provincetown Tennessee Williams Theater Festival Programing 2006–2015..175

Acknowledgments

Over a thousand people collaborated to perform Tennessee Williams' plays in Provincetown from 2006 to 2015. Such support inspires me and I am grateful for it, in particular for the continuing collaboration of Jef Hall-Flavin, now the Festival's executive director (who came to co-direct the world premiere of *The Parade* in our first year) and Charlene Donaghy (a stage manager in our second year) now the Festival's Producing Director. Meg Tracy, the Festival designer for the first four years, continues to offer valuable advice.

I'm indebted to Thomas Keith, who has edited my writing for many years. Brenda Currin has listened to me read multiple drafts of these essays out loud to her for ten years. So has Thomas Sullivan. It was Jef Hall-Flavin's idea to collect them into a book. Jon Hansen's enthusiasm for the idea made such a book possible. The generosity of Josh Andrus and Ride Hamilton makes it possible to share my pleasure in their photographs. Thanks also, to the other photographers whose work is included: Jane Paradise, Ralph

Bassett, Antonis Achilleos—and to the great woodcut master Bill Evaul. Kate Rourke's assistance has made writing possible, as has the generous hospitality in New Orleans of Micki-Beth Stiller and Albert Carey.

Issues of the *Tennessee Williams Annual Review* from 1998 to now, edited by Robert Bray, are a free online resource for those interested in Tennessee Williams. Jacqueline O'Connor's "'Living in this little hotel': Boarders on Borders in Tennessee Williams's Early Short Plays" from Issue 3, 2000 was the seed of The Hotel Plays. Allean Hale's articles "Confronting the Late Plays of Tennessee Williams," Issue 6, 2003 and "Tennessee Williams's Three Plays for the Lyric Theatre" from Issue 7, 2005 were essential to me, and anyone else, interested in staging late Williams. "Tennessee Williams's American Blues: From the Early Manuscripts Through Menagerie" by Nick Moschovakis in the 2005 issue led to the great pleasures of Alison's Fraser's *Tennessee Williams: Words & Music* and the theme of the 2012 festival season. The camaraderie of the New Orleans/Tennessee Williams Theater Festival provided opportunity for direct exchanges of ideas, questions, and more questions with inspiring scholars, among them Annette Saddik, Allean Hale, Karen Kohlhaas, and Kenneth Holditch. For years Peggy Fox, Barbara Epler, and Laurie Callahan of New Directions have offered support and encouragement in New York, as have Tom Erhardt and Mel Kenyon at Casarotto Ramsay in London.

Jerry Stacy makes my life possible.

Introduction: The Talent that Survives

It continues to be remorselessly true that I am placed in the all-but impossible position of having to compete with myself as an emerging young playwright. I could not give you another Menagerie nor Streetcar. I can only give you a thing that I cannot estimate for you, the talent that survives and with it whatever prolonged exercise of my craft may have added to it.

—Tennessee Williams from an unpublished essay, "Mending Sails by Candlelight," written for the Broadway opening of *Clothes for a Summer Hotel*, March 1980.

Since you have opened this book and are taking the time to read this introduction, you likely have some interest in, experience with, curiosity about, or love of the plays of Tennessee Williams. The essays in this volume were all written by David Kaplan in conjunction with the Provincetown Tennessee Williams Theater Festival, of which he is the curator and a co-founder. They are organized in two sections. The first section consists of ten essays written for each year of the Provincetown Festival. Those essays focus on each year's thematic selection of Williams plays—and other dance, music, and theater events—as

Captain Jack's Wharf on the Provincetown Bay. Detail of a charcoal drawing by Bill Evaul, 2012. Tennessee Williams lived at Captain Jack's in 1940, sleeping in the highest unit the first summer he came to Provincetown. In the summer of 1944 Williams stayed at the unit at the end of the wharf facing the bay.

well as some aspect of Williams' plays not always obvious in the text but essential to understanding the plays in production. The second section includes seven occasional essays, written for productions of Williams plays associated with the Festival. All the essays relate, in one way or another, to the story of what happened to the playwright during the last twenty years of his life and how his reputation is evolving since his death.

It has become common enough knowledge, in the theater anyway, that after the Broadway production of *The Night of the Iguana* closed in 1962, Tennessee Williams' reputation and career took a steep dive from which he never recovered, certainly not during his lifetime. After the unhappy Broadway ventures of *The Milk Train Doesn't Stop Here Anymore* in 1963 and 1964, every new play by Williams was burdened by the author's tenuous physical and emotional health, made worse by his drug and alcohol abuse, and battered by the critics in nearly every case: they didn't feel he was relevant; they didn't understand what he was trying to do; and they wanted him to again write the plays that made him famous, which no playwright has ever been able to do. By the mid-1960s, in their frustration and imperiousness, the critics began to review the man more than they reviewed his plays until, by the last two years of his life, they just stopped showing up. It is a singularly ugly story in American theater history and it didn't help that Williams refused to give up, that he kept working to the very end. This meant that after Williams' death in 1983, his reputation remained in perdition, and an entire corpus of unpublished writing (sixteen full-length plays and over thirty one-acts) was dismissed, avoided, forgotten, or unavailable.

While there has never been much critical or popular erosion in the acceptance of his greatest works—especially the big three, *The Glass Menagerie*, *A Streetcar Named Desire*, and *Cat on a Hot Tin Roof*—opinions about the playwright's voluminous output after *Iguana* have been sharp and divergent. Fortunately, those judgments have also evolved and continue to evolve. Whether one views Williams' later plays as the bad plays of a once-great writer, a break into experimentation, a response to the escalating hostility from the critics that started in the late 1950s, a desire to connect with the changing American society of the 1960s and '70s, the outpourings of a man debilitated by drugs and alcohol, part of a continuum of the theatrical vision of a great playwright, or some combination thereof, is mostly academic. Well, it is academic until the plays are seen by audiences: produced, inhabited by actors, engaged by designers, and marshaled as live events by directors. Like all plays on the printed page, they are blueprints; some quite readable and complex as literature, though never fully understood until realized as live theater. The Provincetown Tennessee Williams Theater Festival leadership—David Kaplan, Jef Hall-Flavin, Charlene Donaghy, and Patrick Falco—have made it their business to further expand the ongoing conversation about

Williams' critical reputation by bringing his plays to life without regard to preconceived beliefs about the man or his work.

From the time Williams' one-act play *Moony's Kid Don't Cry* was published in 1940 until his death in 1983, twenty-one full-length plays and thirty-two one-acts were made widely available in print. After his death there was quite a lot of unpublished material to consider and organize—how to bring out the letters and the journals and who should edit them were among the top concerns. Since 1983, fourteen full-length plays and forty-three one-acts have been published, many of them early or juvenile plays, though most were written or finished after 1960. Four post-*Iguana* or "late" plays were issued from 1983 to 1997: *Clothes for a Summer Hotel*; *Tiger Tail*; *Something Cloudy, Something Clear*; and *The Notebook of Trigorin*. Beginning in 1998, five of Williams' earliest full-length plays, known as "the apprentice plays," were published: *Candles to the Sun*; *Fugitive Kind*; *Not About Nightingales*; *Spring Storm*; and *Stairs to the Roof*.

When I was working as an editor full-time for New Directions Publishing in 2002, Peggy Fox, then Vice President of the company and Williams' last editor during his lifetime, turned over to me the responsibility of editing the Tennessee Williams titles. Peggy then charged me with reissuing Williams' "top ten"—his most famous, critically successful plays, originally produced from 1945 to 1961—in new editions with new introductions and new covers. There was also a fair amount of previously unpublished and uncollected material for me to sort out, some of it in progress (such as the letters volumes), but much of it in stasis.

Peggy had already enlisted the talents of scholars Allean Hale and Dan Isaac to prepare the apprentice plays, and Albert Devlin and Nancy Tischler to work on the letters. And, as part of their research for *The Collected Poems of Tennessee Williams*, scholars Nicholas Moschovakis and David Roessel spent a good deal of time in the archives in the Harry Ransom Center at the University of Texas, Austin. While looking for poems they came upon quite a few one-acts, primarily early or juvenile, that were complete, unpublished, unproduced, and unknown, outside of mentions in letters and journal entries. When Nick and David brought those plays to the attention of director Michael Kahn at the Shakespeare Theatre Company in Washington D.C.—Kahn knew Williams from directing the hugely successful 1974 revival of *Cat on Hot Tin Roof* on Broadway and the revised version of *Kingdom of Earth* at the McCarter Theater—he immediately saw their potential and put together an evening of the "new" one-acts as part of the Kennedy Center's 2004 summer tribute to Williams. The evening was so successful that it moved, with a few adjustments, to the Manhattan Theater Club in New York City that fall. The success of these early and unknown plays in production, on their feet so to speak, provided the impetus for me to make a case for their publication. The result was the 2005 publication of *Mister Paradise and Other*

One-Act Plays, edited, with notes and an introduction, by Nick and David. The volume also includes two plays from the 1960s, *And Tell Sad Stories of the Deaths of Queens*…and *The Municipal Abattoir*.

In 2004, theater director David Kaplan met with the Board of Directors of the Provincetown Theater to discuss how the town's new theater space—a former garage that was refurbished as a theater in 2001—might be best used. The suggestions of a children's theater, the home for a dance company, and a Portuguese language theater were all rejected but as soon as Kaplan proposed a Tennessee Williams Theater Festival, the consensus was unanimous that it *might* be a good idea. Publicist Lynne Kortenhaus thought it was a brilliant idea. The next evening, six people met for dinner to discuss the nuts and bolts of the idea: theater director David Kaplan; owner of the Waterford Inn Jerry Scally; owner of the *Provincetown Banner* Alix Ritchie; and their significant others. Shortly thereafter, they brought in local theater director Patrick Falco and began putting things in motion for a Festival launch in 2006. One of the first things the organizers did was attend the Tennessee Williams Festivals in New Orleans, Louisiana, and in Clarksdale and Columbus, Mississippi, to meet people and to find out and learn from what others were already doing. Their festival in Provincetown would have to serve a new purpose. It would become the first theater festival dedicated to full productions of Williams plays.

The excitement surrounding the discovery of the early one-acts in *Mister Paradise*, opened the door for consideration of some of the later plays that had proven more problematic and prompted me to offer a plan for their publication. While the rediscovered one-acts were playing at the Kennedy Center in 2004 and being edited for publication, David Kaplan and his comrades were planning the first Provincetown Tennessee Williams Theater Festival. At about the same time, I invited scholar Annette Saddik, whom I had met at the Tennessee Williams New Orleans/Literary Festival, to edit a collection of late Williams plays, most of those manuscripts already in the New Directions files, published in 2008 as *The Traveling Companion and Other Plays*. That volume turned out to be closely tied to the Provincetown Festival: five of the twelve plays, *The Parade, The Pronoun 'I', The Remarkable Rooming-House of Mme. Le Monde, Green Eyes,* and *Sunburst,* had their world premiere productions at the Provincetown Festival; *The Day on Which a Man Dies* premiered in Chicago, directed by David Kaplan; and three others, *The Chalky White Substance, The One Exception,* and *The Traveling Companion* have been produced by the Festival.

Producing these primarily unknown later works in Provincetown was often a revelation, beginning with *The Parade* in 2006. Sketched by Williams in August of 1940, at the end of his first summer in Provincetown, *The Parade* is the author's response to falling in love for the first time and then feeling the sting of rejection. Williams fleshed out his notes, writing the play in 1962, and he made further revisions when he prepared the text to be submitted by his agent for publication in 1979 as part of a folder of odds and ends titled "Pieces of My Youth." Waiting all those years in a file drawer at New Directions, *The Parade* was the centerpiece of the Festival's first season and the subject of a *New York Times* article by Randy Gener about the unabashed rendering of gay characters in this unassuming play begun sixty-six years earlier. With few stage directions and little by way of traditional structure, it was not at all certain that the dusty script would work as a play. Yet on stage, co-directed by Jef Hall-Flavin and Eric Powell Holm, *The Parade* turned out to be a deeply stirring portrait of unrequited love infused with an artist's longing to create. It plays beautifully.

George Bixby, the proprietor of a private, limited edition publishing firm called Albondocani Press (1968–1991), contacted Tennessee Williams' agent in 1982 with a request to bring out a signed, limited edition of the one-act play, *The Traveling Companion*, which had been published the previous year in the gay literary magazine *Christopher Street*. When I spoke with Mr. Bixby in 2007, he explained that Williams communicated through the agent that he would prefer a different new play be published instead and sent along a copy of *The Remarkable Rooming-House of Mme. Le Monde*, which was published in a limited edition in 1984. It was not an accident that the short play Williams offered to Bixby is not only of an experimental nature, but also a darkly comic, violent, cartoonish, and overtly sexual caper. It goes farther into the realm of difficult and late Williams than any other play previously encountered by the public. The scene: the attic of a London rooming-house that is "equipped with curved metal hooks which provide the little man [Mint, the tenant] a means of locomotion, as his legs are mysteriously paralyzed and his hands swing from hook to hook." At the opening of the play, Mint is behind an opaque curtain being sodomized by one of Mme. Le Monde's muscular offspring who finishes quickly, leaving Mint to plead, "Put me back on a hook, please, please, put me back on a hook before my guest arrives for tea." As things get more violent and more hilarious by turns, the action is accompanied throughout, like a British music hall act, with a tinny recording of "Tea For Two." Williams identified the style as Guignol. The play was begging to be performed, but both the theatrical agent for Williams at the time, Tom Erhardt, and the organizers of the Provincetown Festival knew that they had to find the right company to perform it and the right person to direct it; a director who could mine the text for all its horrors, let the humor soar, and not impose anything that would constitute rewriting or misinterpreting the world premiere of a Tennessee Williams play. Fortunately for the play and the Festival, Davis Robinson and the Beau Jest Moving Theatre were available in 2009. Remaining true to the text, Robinson and his company solved perplexing technical challenges and mustered a balance of styles, Gothic and slapstick. Robinson and the Beau Jest Moving Theatre proved that the play works. What audiences may think of it is another matter; however, in Provincetown, the response was a mixture of awe and guffaw. Approached with preconceptions about the value or quality of Williams' later plays, *The Remarkable Rooming-House of Mme. Le Monde* would not likely have much of a life.

The negative reviews of original productions of Williams' late work tend to follow those plays through the years to reviewers of productions decades later who will sometimes lazily quote the old reviews and jauntily belly up to the bar of contempt so they won't have to read the play or do any original thinking. Or worse, reviewers will cite the personal problems of the playwright at the time he wrote a given play as a reason for a contemporary audience to dismiss it. Critics lambasted *Kingdom of Earth* when it opened on Broadway in 1968, under the title *The Seven Descents of Myrtle*, calling it "a disappointment," "tired," and "a joke," among many other things. As recently as August 2015, a reviewer writing about the inaugural production of the Tennessee Williams Theatre Company of New Orleans referred to *Kingdom of Earth* as "bad Williams" and another cited the failure of the original production as a reason why the play should not be produced. Is there bad Shakespeare? Bad Ibsen? Bad O'Neill? Sure, but we don't think of it that way; each playwright wrote a number of plays taken as their body of work. The matter of an individual play being bad or good, early or late, is less relevant than its inherent dramatic, textual, or theatrical value. *Hamlet* may be the crown of the Bard's brilliance, but that doesn't mean *Cymbeline* should be simply discarded as "bad."

So where can one find a theater company that will approach the late work of Tennessee Williams with entirely fresh eyes? One of the many places to turn is Cape Town, South Africa. Tom Erhardt suggested *Kingdom of Earth* to Fred Abrahamse and Marcel Meyers, of Abrahamse/Meyers Productions. Fred and Marcel took on *Kingdom of Earth* in 2012 without having visited the Mississippi Delta, without experiencing racism in America, without living on a flood plain, without hearing American Southern accents, and without bias. They brought to the work an understanding of how to tell a story, the experience of coming from a country with an inexorable history of racial divisions, and the curiosity to excavate all their choices from the text itself. The result was a production of the play that was so electric and surprising that many of the people who saw it, myself included, felt that we'd seen a new play—or at least a play we'd never fully understood before. This was a different kind of revelation and, as with other productions at the Festival, it was fidelity to the text and an effort to understand Williams' intentions that made it so exciting. Director Abrahamse made no impositions on the playwright or his work, but rather found a story within *Kingdom of Earth* that was waiting to be told. And there will be other interpretations, hopefully discovered with the same ferocious care. For most of the English-speaking world, Williams' oeuvre is not divided in half, nor categorized as good or bad. As Marcel Meyers has written, "Tennessee Williams *is* and always *was* a great playwright. Period. He wasn't good up to a point and then suddenly became a bad playwright." Abrahamse and Meyers have since brought smart and dynamic productions of Williams' *The Milk Train Doesn't Stop Here Anymore* and Yukio Mishima's modern Noh play *The Lady Aoi* to Provincetown.

Discovering how Williams plays play on the stage, the famous and the not-so-famous and even the "bad," is part of an ongoing conversation that will affect Williams' reputation over time. The productions in Provincetown have been part of this conversation for the last ten years, as have the companies with which the Festival collaborates. Those companies, arriving at the Festival from around the country and around the globe—Minnesota, Kansas, Ohio, Michigan, New Mexico, New Hampshire, New York, England, Italy, Portugal, South Africa, and New Zealand, to name a few locations—have also entered the conversation, continue it, and take it home with them. And when they bring their work to Provincetown they find the performance spaces are rarely traditional: Sarah Michaelson's six-person *Camino Real* enacted on a wharf at dusk; one-acts revitalized by David Kaplan, Davis Robinson, Patrick Falco, and Jef Hall-Flavin on porches and in cramped hotel rooms; David Kaplan's site-adapted presentation of *The Day on Which a Man Dies* in a gallery of the Provincetown Art Museum; Cosmin Chivu's windswept production of *Something Cloudy, Something Clear* in a tent on a beach; Patrick Falco's boisterous *The Case of the Crushed Petunias* outside and inside a Commercial Street store front; Jef Hall-Flavin's production of *A Lovely Sunday for Creve Coeur* achieved inside a private home; Cosmin Chivu's peripatetic rendition of *The Mutilated* traveling through the Gifford House; and Nick Potenzieri's investigation of *Orpheus Descending* in two different Provincetown churches. Frequently site-adapted, sometimes site-specific, the experiences are distinguished by the innovative use of unexpected spaces, which inform the plays and expand the vocabulary of the audiences.

It's not only the theatrical vocabulary that audiences in Provincetown develop; they have learned, over ten years, to appreciate the works-in-progress, to take in unfamiliar Williams plays without inflexible assumptions about the life of the playwright. And, as their knowledge of Williams increases, they have a keener perspective. Audiences in Provincetown now expect the unexpected and, by remaining open to possibilities, they are rewarded with theater experiences and a fresh perspective on Tennessee Williams.

During the ten years the Provincetown Festival has been up and running, a third volume of previously unpublished uncollected one-acts, *The Magic Tower and Other One-Act Plays*, was published, as were Williams' last full-length play, *A House Not Meant to Stand*, a reissue of Williams' *Memoirs* with an introduction by John Waters, and an expanded collection of the playwright's essays, edited by John S. Bak. Productions of Williams' late, later, lesser-known, and more experimental and presentational plays have sprung up all over the country, and there have been premieres of some of his plays in London, Boston, Minneapolis, Chicago, Toronto, and New Orleans. The Provincetown Tennessee Williams Theater Festival has hosted a series of special guests, all of whom have a strong connection with Williams and many who knew him well: John Guare, Amiri Baraka, Mia Phoebus (Ethel Elkovsky), Olympia Dukakis, Anne Jackson, Eli Wallach, Lanford Wilson, William Jay Smith, Lee Breuer, Mitch Douglas, and John Lahr.

Now you have some background about where the Provincetown Festival fits into the past and the future of Williams' plays and his evolving reputation. In the following essays, David Kaplan will take you deeper into how the plays of Tennessee Williams work—some you already know and some that will be new to you—and how they found their way off the page and on to the many stages of the Tennessee Williams Provincetown Theater Festival.

Thomas Keith
September 2015

TENN YEARS

The Annual Festival Essays

2006

Tennessee Williams in Provincetown

There was no catalog essay for the Provincetown Tennessee Williams Theater Festival in 2006. There was no catalog. That year, the first year of the Festival, audiences were handed a legal-size piece of paper with credits for the show they were watching. The next few years there were feisty newsprint booklets. Those had essays. In 2010 the catalog paper turned glossy.

In 2006, what there was to say about the Festival programming was on the Festival website and in press releases. There were a dozen events over four days: plays, dances, live music, and films. All the events were connected in some way to Tennessee Williams' time in Provincetown.

If there had been such a thing as a catalog in 2006, and there had been a catalog essay in it, the essay would have pointed out that plays Williams worked on in Provincetown were returning to the Cape—and from unexpected places. Plays he'd written in the 1940s at Captain Jack's Wharf, and in a dune shack, and in an

Tennessee Williams in Provincetown, 1944. Detail of a photograph in the Provincetown dunes. Photo courtesy of Joe Hazan.

East End beach house, were being performed six decades later by actors from the Hong Kong Repertory Theater, the Provincetown High School, college students from Sewanee, Tennessee and Starkville, Mississippi, sung by singers from Capitol City Opera of Atlanta, Georgia and danced as a ballet under the supervision of Lowell Smith from the Dance Theater of Harlem.

A 2006 catalog essay would have touted that in Provincetown, because of its history (Pilgrim, Portuguese, 1920s radicals, 1930s émigrés, late-1960s hippies, mid-1970s gay, all those histories), because of its social liberties (religious, racial, artistic, political, sexual, all those liberties) and because of its audience (fishing families, artists, theater-going Bostonians and New Yorkers, all those people sitting together) aspects of Williams writing and life could be uniquely understood, performed, and appreciated at this small New England village surrounded by water on three sides.

In 1940, Williams fell in love in Provincetown, and had his heart broken, too, by a green-eyed Canadian dancer who called himself Kip. Sixty-six years later we produced the world premiere of a play Williams began at the time about his broken heart—*The Parade* or *Approaching the End of a Summer*—in which being gay is called as normal as a duck's egg. Williams' diary entries from his time in Provincetown inspired a dance in 2006, performed on Fisherman's Wharf by Bennington College students, with the bay doors of the wharf-house pulled open so that the water could be seen as a backdrop. The wind played a major role, rustling the costumes and the dancers' hair and the audience, whipping up the white cloth wrapped around Kip, who died of a brain tumor. The audience wept.

A catalog essay would have announced our mission to "encourage the searching spirit of Williams' writing to inspire new creative work." At the Provincetown Theater, the company bravely called The New Provincetown Players was showing fourteen new short plays written by local playwrights based on themes from Williams. Around the corner at the artSTRAND Gallery there was a collaboration called *The Foggy Foggy Dew* between seminal Provincetown sculptor/painter Jim Peters and Obie-winning playwright Wendy Kesselman. At what was then called The Vixen we presented a staged reading of Ryan Landry's unfinished *Plexiglas Menagerie*, the last (so far) in a series of Williams drag parodies Landry had been writing for years.

A catalog essay wouldn't have said so, but the 2006 line-up hinted at themes and preoccupations for years to come: Williams' classics, like *The Glass Menagerie*, alongside a world premiere, like *The Parade*, unexpected multi-ethnic casting, women directors, choreographers, and playwrights, adaptations of Williams' work—including his poetry—in music and dance. The 2007 programming was already planned, with an emphasis on the wilder Williams: what he wrote after he turned sixty. We were committed to developing new plays. Both *The Foggy Foggy Dew* and *The Plexiglas Menagerie* received full productions in 2007.

From the beginning, the hope was that audience members would see everything on the year's program—or if not everything, at least enough to realize that everything was connected in some way to that year's theme. The idea was that different approaches to Williams plays would ricochet off each other in the audience's imagination to a further understanding of the playwright's range and depth. From 2005, even before the festival began, annual themes were planned to spin out of each other, in some ways countering the theme that had come before and what would come after. The 2008 theme, for example, *The Healing Power of Love*, contained the 2009 counter-theme, *The Fight for Life*, which was itself countered by 2010's focus on influence, what Williams gained from what surrounded him rather than what he had to struggle to oppose.

A 2006 catalog essay, if there had been one, would have pointed out a door had opened in Provincetown for Tennessee Williams in 1940, just as a door opened at a wharf house for the first performance on our first day in 2006. Williams fell in love in Provincetown, found heartbreak there. He met superstars of German art there: Hans Hofmann and Valeska Gert. He met Jackson Pollock here (through Lee Krasner, who was studying with Hofmann). The theme for 2007, *The Late Late Show*, would demonstrate that the same door opened again when Williams grew older, that in his most daring experiments he was walking back through the door, seeing something simultaneously new and old. Every year since, such a door has opened and the catalog essay has tried to open new doors, too, to what we might think of as the bay that leads out into the oceanic Tennessee Williams.

2007

The Late Late Show

The Remarkable Rooming-House of Mme. Le Monde, the world premiere production from the Beau Jest Moving Theatre Company of Boston. Directed by David Robertson, Jordan Harrison as Mint, Larry Coen as Hall, TW Fest 2009. The production began a change in the critical reception of late Williams. Photo by Justin Knight.

I think the strange, the crazed, the queer
Will have their holiday this year
 —Tennessee Williams, from the unpublished "Poem for Paul"

Tennessee Williams' public success began in late 1944 with the critical acclamation of *The Glass Menagerie* in Chicago, the approval sustained and supportive enough to make it a hit despite a snowstorm. The subsequent Broadway production of *Glass Menagerie* three months later in March, confirmed Williams' popularity with audiences and critics, over-riding the reservations of the then significant but not yet all-powerful *New York Times*. The playwright was just thirty-four-years old. Nine months before he had been living in an unheated shack in the dunes of Provincetown.

Williams' reputation ascended through Broadway productions of *A Streetcar Named Desire* (1947), *Summer and Smoke* (1948), *The Rose Tattoo* (1951), *Cat on a Hot Tin Roof* (1955), *and The Night of Iguana* (1961). He was awarded the Pulitzer Prize twice, for

Streetcar and *Cat*. What few unpopular and unconventional works he presented—*Camino Real* (1953) and *Period of Adjustment* (1960)—were dismissed as aberrational stumbling. Beginning in 1962, however, Williams' writing insistently took on forms that conventional critics and Broadway audiences were no longer willing to approve, applaud, or attend.

In early 1963 and again in 1964, *The Milk Train Doesn't Stop Here Anymore* tanked. His double-bill on Broadway, *Slapstick Tragedy* (*The Mutilated* and *The Gnädiges Fräulein*), closed in 1966 after six days. After *In the Bar of a Tokyo Hotel* opened Off-Broadway in 1969 it was viciously attacked. *Life* magazine, more interested in the playwright than the play, diagnosed he had "suffered an infantile progression from which there seems no exit." The "Life Theater Review" with its headline "White Dwarf's Tragic Fade-out" was placed opposite an advertisement for canned vegetables with its headline "Our beans won't go limp."

In 1969, Williams could be said to have hit bottom when he sat on a stove in his Key West home and ended up with third degree burns. A danger to himself and to others, he was packed away by his younger brother to a St. Louis hospital and taken off booze and pills. Two heart attacks and a seizure followed. He emerged with a long beautiful poem, which reveals his self-awareness in extremis and his ability to anneal even the most painful of experiences into powerful writing. The title was lifted from a question asked by a night-nurse:

"What's Next on the Agenda, Mr. Williams?"

What was next on the agenda was over a dozen years of writing and over two dozen plays that sabotaged the certainties of memory and knowledge, and the certainties of good taste, recklessly undermining his earlier reputation for greatness.

In 1971, after he turned sixty, Tennessee Williams wrote at least twenty-four plays, six of them full-length. He finished several long-range writing projects. *Vieux Carré*, performed on Broadway in 1977 in New York, had been brewing since 1941 when he proposed an evening of three short plays all set in the French Quarter under that title. *Something Cloudy, Something Clear*, which opened in downtown Manhattan at the Jean Cocteau Repertory Theatre in 1981, relied on memories of Provincetown from the summer of 1940. At the time of Williams' death, in February 1983, several other long-range projects were in draft form and he had new ideas for new plays—left in various stages of completion: notes, scenes, finished and unfinished drafts. On the evidence of the papers stored in the archives at Harvard Theatre Collection in Cambridge, Massachusetts, the Harry Ransom Humanities and Research Center in Austin, Texas, and other places, Williams wrote at least as much in his sixties as any other decade of his adult life.

Throughout the same dozen years, he completed his *Memoirs*, a collection of short stories, a novel, a screenplay, and a volume of poetry.

Conservative critics derided what they considered his deteriorating craft. Young and upcoming critics attacked his old-fashioned ways, lack of political commitment, or inappropriate personal candor. These younger critics hurt him deeply. In late June of 1975, the eighteen-year-old Annette Cardona, who was the ingénue in *The Red Devil Battery Sign*, found him sobbing in the lobby over bad reviews in Boston. The town had treated him badly in 1940 when his first Broadway-bound play, *Battle of Angels*, closed there due to bad reviews and censors. Puritans who wanted to find a moral lesson in Williams' life could connect his failure to please the public, or the critics, with his public drunkenness, drug use, and sexual promiscuity. Liberation theorists who wanted to find a psychological lesson in his life could connect his failure with self-loathing, which to them explained the lack of positive gay role models in his plays

Playwrights present fictional lives that have form, meaning, significance, and poetry. It is difficult not to try to give the playwright's own life some form, meaning, significance, and poetry. It is very hard not to do that with Williams, and perhaps we shouldn't try to avoid seeing a design for his life in a story or a poem or a play. He was, when all is said and done, writing mythology, living a myth, and he himself knew he had mythic role models. In the early 1940s he had imagined a poet living in obscurity in the French Quarter whose dreams had never come to be. Biographies of his life have made a three-act drama out of his life: apprentice years; maturity; long, slow decline. There is a counter-biography, too: experimenter; conformist; outsider who alternates between wanting inclusion and not caring anymore. It is easy enough to read in his diaries and letters that after he turned a certain age he no longer saw the world in the same way as he had seen the world when he was younger. Another possible narrative, based on reading his plays closely, is that his departure from realism had always been there, to lesser or greater degrees. Williams began as a poet and throughout his dramatic work poetry dissolves dramatic form. Any and all of these stories of his life are interpretations. Let's stick with the plays themselves.

> "I am quite through with the kind of play that established my early and popular reputation. I am doing a different thing, which is altogether my own, not influenced at all by other playwrights at home or abroad, or by other schools of theatre." (Tennessee Williams, "Foreword" to *Memoirs*)

From 1962 on, the playwright brought forward elements of his work that seemed to repudiate the writing for which he had previously been praised. Stops in the flow of the spoken word—broken rhythms, unfinished sentences and dropped words—

thwarted the expectations of audiences waiting for the liquid cadence and extended lyric passages of the early plays. The later plays that were performed—*Clothes for a Summer Hotel* (1980); *The Milk Train Doesn't Stop Here Anymore* (1964);*The Eccentricities of a Nightingale* (1965); *In the Bar of a Tokyo Hotel* (1969); *Small Craft Warnings* (1972); *The Red Devil Battery Sign* (1975); *Something Cloudy, Something Clear* (1981), and others—plots that went unresolved, subject matter sure to displease, unwelcome political insight, an increasing paranoia rather than confidence. There was a conspicuous lack of comforting realism or recognizable representations of America, replaced by unsettling cartoonish and hallucinatory portraits. Plays that were finished by Williams, and even published, but not performed in public, *The Remarkable Rooming-House of Mme. Le Monde* (1982), for example, are cruel comedies, often concluding with sardonically happy endings.

While Williams' work after 1962 dissolved conventional plot and characterization and taunted expectations of realism and good taste, there was a counter-trend by Williams to investigate the aspects of the seminal realistic playwrights—Chekhov, Strindberg and Ibsen—writers Williams had studied as models since college. Reviewing these masters, at a time of his own mastery, Williams found confirmation of his own preoccupations in the paranoiac humor of Strindberg, the embracing of love in all forms of Chekhov and, from Ibsen, an assault on conventional institutions, without offering up a plan of action in response, beyond a call for personal integrity.

The craft and style of his younger self was not sufficient to convey his mature experience and sharpened insights. He grew to distrust conclusions—about life and in plays. Not even his dead remained dead to him. The multiple exposures of past, present, and future appear on stage in his later plays as séances, hallucinations, and ghosts. He thought again about familiar subject matter. His sister Rose, whose crippling madness and lobotomy had seemed unbearably pitiful before, commanded respect for her obdurate grace. The women depicted in his late plays who reflect his sister—sometimes mad, and often fragile—no longer depend on the kindness of strangers, they depend—however fitfully—on themselves. Over time, Williams' sense of his own strength as a marginalized gay man turned political and his critique of society grew fierce. As early as 1965 he denounced the Viet Nam War as "incredibly cruel: believe me, nothing that will be won out of this war will be worth the life of a single man who died in it." *The Red Devil Battery Sign*, written in 1975, fantasized about a Texas cabal of corrupt politicians in cahoots with war profiteers.

Some of Williams' work was so defiant of social or dramatic conventions of his time—either unacceptably homosexual or anarchic in form—that he hid some of his writing from his agents and kept manuscripts for his own purposes rather than public performance or publication. Famously, in 1971 he dismissed his long-term agent, Audrey Wood, who had been representing him since 1939. Miss Wood somehow persuaded the author to stay within the firm, ICM, and a succession of young men: Bill Barnes, Mitch Douglas, and Luis Sanjurjo, brought the writer's work downtown to the experimental Cocteau Repertory Theater and to the openly gay *Christopher Street* magazine. This refocusing of Williams' energies from Broadway to The Truck and Warehouse Theatre (for the world premiere of *Small Craft Warnings*), from the heterosexual mainstream *Playboy* Magazine (for the exuberantly heterosexual saga of "Miss Coynte of Green") to the proudly homosexual *Christopher Street* Magazine (for the hilarious story of "The Killer Chicken and the Closet Queen") further antagonized those who were bent on maintaining the prestige of mainstream venues. The change of Williams' directors from establishment figures such as Elia Kazan and José Quintero to upstarts like Eve Adamson and Keith Hack was also a change in professional status that was seen, correctly, as a repudiation of past standards.

> What moves men of genius, or rather, what inspires their work, is not new ideas, but their obsession with the idea that what has already been said is still not enough. (Eugene Delacroix's journal, May 15, 1824)

Williams' late plays have an aesthetic of their own: what we might call Tennessee Williams' Late Late show. To begin with, there are the broken rhythms of the words, very different than the mellifluous flow of his earlier successes. The punctuation, something Williams was punctilious about (unlike his spelling) involves a lot of dashes and ellipses. This jagged surface rhythm was often stupidly assigned to an inability to finish sentences because it was presumed he was drunk or stoned (as if El Greco's lengthened figure were due to eye disease) or even more ignorantly it was attributed to some sort of psychological impotency which is hard to reconcile with the massive output. So many of these writings were kept private, it can be difficult to say with finality exactly what he wrote between 1962 and 1983. The most recent estimate is maybe sixty plays.

Give the respect due to such a great artist: his discordant music is not unlike the discordant music of composers who, like Williams, early in youth found success with soothing melodies. Beethoven, Scriabin, and Shostakovich, all turned on their early successes and quoted themselves ironically in tilted waltzes and broken chords. Disharmony expressed what they experienced in the world. The broken rhythms of late Williams did the same. Manet and Picasso also turned on their earlier sweetness. Theater critics, notoriously behind the times, wanted Williams to continue his Rose period and his Blue Period.

There is crudeness to some of his late plays; the playwright has something more urgent to say than good taste will allow. In

Kirche, Küche, Kinder (1979)—a play we're not showing this year because no professional theater we approached would consider it—a father is sending his children out into the world and instructs them pull down their pants so he may inspect their privates, since that, after all is what he is raising them to sell.

Such plays, on the rare occasions they were staged, were condescended to by reviewers—and their author was belittled. Heroically Williams wrote on. His short-sighted critics have passed from power; the willful executor of his estate who put the kibosh on his openly gay writing—and life-story—passed away in 1994. The texts remain. A more savvy estate has agreed to their publication. Many of these late plays rely, however, not on the printed or spoken word, but on what's acted out: the arrival of a prop, a hand gesture, the sight of a naked body next to a clothed one. An audience's response is essential to the effect of these plays in performance: beginning with the reflex of sharing a hard loud laugh.

The Remarkable Rooming-House of Mme. Le Monde, *in an early draft, was titled "A Rectangle with Hooks." Larry Coen as Hall. Photo by Jane Paradise.*

2008

The Healing Power of Love

A vision of love informs what Tennessee Williams wrote the way the weather in a growing season informs the taste of that year's wine. We write about what we know—or think we know—and Williams' knowledge of love, as with us all, is rooted in first experience. His mother's fierce and toxic love shimmers in *The Glass Menagerie*, the play that began his successful Broadway career. The first man he fell in love with, Kip Kiernan, who fired and cracked Williams' heart for all time in the space of three weeks in Provincetown, is reflected in *The Glass Menagerie's* Gentleman Caller gently breaking off any chance that first love might last more than a night.

Further experience informed Williams' understanding of love and ways to write about it. In 1946, Amado "Pancho" Rodriquez y Gonzales, the son of a Mexican border-guard, moved into Williams' New Orleans apartment—Pancho twenty-four to Williams' thirty-four. It was the first time either man formed such a bond. Williams and Pancho held different ideals of fidelity; the consequences

A moment of reconciliation in The Mutilated, *Beth Bartley Productions / InterArt Group, New York City. Mink Stole as Trinket and Penny Arcade as Celeste, directed by Cosmin Chivu. TW Fest 2013. Photo by Josh Andrus.*

resonate in the plays Williams was writing. In *A Streetcar Named Desire*, domesticity cohabits with violence, love is a narcotic and a balm; in *Summer and Smoke* a southern gentleman dallies with a Mexican temptress before abandoning her for a conventional life in town. Beneath the turbulent surface of both plays there's a Mexican undertow. Guitars and mariachi bands play in the distance, Mexican vendors whisper subtext in the street, spoken Spanish is the language of tenderness and passion. How well did Williams understand Spanish or for that matter Pancho? As Miss Alma (the word for "soul" in Spanish) explains in *Summer and Smoke* to a traveling salesman she picks up in the square, "Sometimes *un poquito* is enough."

Summering in Provincetown with Pancho in 1947, Williams met Frank Merlo on the porch of the A-House. Merlo was twenty-five, just out of the Navy, a Sicilian-American from New Jersey with inviting shoulders and a jaw like a nutcracker. After the inevitable break with Pancho, and time out to find himself in Italy, Williams reconnected with Frank when they ran into each other at an all-night deli in Manhattan. Pancho blazed in Williams' life for two years. Merlo was a steadier burn, making a home with Williams in Key West. Despite Williams' habitual pleasure-seeking, the Merlo-Williams connection lasted fourteen years, until Frank died of lung cancer. *The Rose Tattoo*—dedicated "To Frank In Return For Sicily" (where they traveled together in 1949)—overflows with an abundance of heart more than any other work by Williams. As the play was being formed, Williams' close friendship with the Italian actress Anna Magnani revealed to him that love was as much earth as air. A bottle of chianti, distilled from intimacies with Merlo or Magnani, stands on the nightstand of the one-night stand in *The Eccentricities of a Nightingale*—a recommendation for that play's Miss Alma to seize happiness when she can.

When the young hustler in *The Traveling Companion* (written two years before Williams passed away) says "I know, I known Italians" the older writer, an obvious Williams self-portrait, retorts "Then I would say you have lived."

Life and love were sometimes unkind to Williams, and Williams was sometimes unkind to himself. For all his born gifts and hard-won accomplishments he was plagued with self-doubt and depression. The guilt he took on for being absent when his sister most needed him, his self-abuse with pills and liquor, his painful reliving of when Kip rejected him—and every other rejection in life—brewed what Williams called his blue devils, even during times in his life when happiness seemed possible and deserved.

His defense, as always, was to write and the words he put down are incantatory:

We are together, breathing quietly together, leaning together quietly, quietly together, completely, sweetly together, not frightened, now, not alone, but completely quietly, together…

(from *Camino Real*)

The sound of this, and its sense, subdued the playwright's devils and renews our own psychic health. In none of his plays, though, is love an end-state. It is a respite, an oasis. It heals, but it does not cure. For Williams, when vision falters and love fades it enhances the worth of vision and love. What's seen in passing before it passes away and what's enjoyed on the wing (including time-out to rest), compels Williams to direct the audience's attention to inevitable loss and our defense against it: love. As Casanova announces on the Camino Real:

For what is the heart but a sort of—a sort of—*instrument*— that translates *noise* into *music*, chaos into—*order*…

A mother tries to comfort her troubled son in Auto-da-Fé. *Cristine McMurdo-Wallis as Mme. Duvenet, Ben Berry as her son Eloi, directed by Jef Hall-Flavin. TW Fest 2012. Photo by Josh Andrus.*

2009

The Fight for Life

The fragile beauty of *The Glass Menagerie* on stage and the tremulous performance of Vivien Leigh in the film version of *A Streetcar Named Desire* both capture one's imagination so thoroughly that the fierce power of their author, Tennessee Williams, is occasionally obscured by the delicacy of his writing.

Yet, Tennessee Williams, in his person and in his personal life, was neither tremulous nor delicate, nor were the men he loved. His work ethic and life-view were vigorous. He had powerful adversaries: poverty, depression, hypochondria, alcohol, pills, and public disgrace. He fought them all to the finish. The Mississippi-born playwright came of age during the Depression and came to maturity during World War II. The experience of living through the Depression and the war shaped his mind and his habits—as much as living in the South and living with his family did—and provided a vocabulary for Williams to explain his family and his heritage to himself and to others.

A Streetcar Named Desire, Jude Gibson as Blanche DuBois, Fortune Theatre Trust, Dunedin, New Zealand, directed by Jef Hall-Flavin. TW Fest 2009. Photo by Jane Paradise.

In 1929 Williams was eighteen, living in St. Louis. The immediate effect on his family from that October's stock market crash was his father's inability to continue paying for his studies at the University of Missouri. Tom, not yet Tennessee, shuffled between three more colleges before graduating in 1938 from the University of Iowa with a dubious asset for getting a job, a degree in English. For the next six years he led a nomadic life. His familiarity with boarding houses, the unemployed, and the desperately employed was acquired.

At the time his most probable source of income, as a writer, was the WPA, the Works Progress Administration. This federal program was founded in 1932 to assist those who were unemployed. Support in Congress to fund unemployed writers—and the arts in general—involved the rationale that American arts aided the common good by boosting morale and articulating American identity. Williams never did work for the WPA as a writer, but the hope of a government paycheck—at this time in his life—led him to believe in theater that tackled social improvement head-on. This was reinforced when Williams moved to New York and fell in with the leftist politics of the professionals he met: the Group Theater, Clifford Odets, and the great German director Erwin Piscator with whom he studied at the New School.

An economic boom arrived with the oncoming world war. The WPA was discontinued, but its rhetoric—of pulling together and working for a common cause—continued, this time applied to the war, and the discipline necessary to wage it. Though America waited to enter battle until December 1941, anyone in Provincetown in 1940, which included Williams, could see that America was preparing to fight. Convoys to support Canadian ships en route to Europe steamed out of the Provincetown port. Airplanes practiced dive bombs in the bay, an armada assembled in the harbor rehearsed formations. When the Japanese attacked Pearl Harbor, the WPA artists, paid for by the government, were set to work promoting the need for discipline, silence, and hard work. Books were promoted as weapons.

What Williams did, on his own, was to take the words and phrases advocating aggression and redeploy them to advocate for creation. From the mouths of several characters in different plays, often life-scarred Jeremiahs with faith in the future, the call went out. The war *for* life, not against it, is what he called it. In *Mister Paradise,* written circa 1940, the poet Anthony Paradise, living in anonymous squalor in the French Quarter of New Orleans, vehemently announces that no one is interested in poetry these days, but just as vehemently passes on his belief:

> There's an end to everything, even to supplies of gunpowder. When they're exhausted people will start looking again under broken table legs for little volumes of forgotten verse.

In *The Case of the Crushed Petunias,* written in 1941, a salesmen comes to a notions store in Primandproper, Massachusetts to urge the proprietress stock up for something other than war:

> Life Incorporated has come to the realization that we have to use the same aggressive methods of promotion used by DEATH, UNLIMITED.

Even before America entered WWII, Williams had a vision of theater after war. In a letter to William Saroyan dated November 29, 1941, one week before Pearl Harbor, Williams wrote: "I think there is going to be a vast hunger for life after all this death—and for light after all this eclipse—People will want to read, see, feel the living truth."

In 1945, with Hiroshima and Auschwitz in the news, *You Touched Me!*, Williams' and his friend Donald Windham's stage adaptation of a short story by D.H. Lawrence, opened on Broadway. The play includes this impassioned speech:

> A new war's beginning….The war for life, not against it. The war to create a world that can live without war. All the dead bodies of Europe, all of the corpses of Africa, Asia, America ought to be raised on flagpoles over the world, and the cities not built up but left as they are—a shambles, a black museum—for you and you and you—to stroll about in—

on Sunday afternoons—in case you forget—and leave the world to chance, and the rats of advantage.

For Williams, that life itself was a battle remained a world-view well after the war and the Depression concluded. As a playwright, Williams' conception of embattled lives on stage was inspired by a lifelong study of the writing of the Swedish master August Strindberg.

Strindberg was born in 1849 and died in 1912. He was at the front of the Scandinavian avant-garde that included the Expressionist painter Edvard Munch and Strindberg's rival, the great playwright Henrik Ibsen. Although Strindberg's plays are often ironically funny, he depicts relationships between men and women as an inevitably violent war. A mythological understanding of the world, which Strindberg shared with Edvard Munch, divided people into vampires or their victims acting out a psychology of eat or be eaten.

To focus an audience on the subtleties of realistic behavior, as signs of internal action—in particular what he called *soul-murder*—Strindberg crafted chamber plays to be performed in intimate spaces.

Miss Julie (*Froken Julie*) a chamber play written by Strindberg in 1888, is considered one of the master works of such drama, or any drama from any period. A synopsis reveals the play's immediate parallels with Williams' *Streetcar:* an aristocratic woman falls for a lower class man, he degrades her, she self-destructs. In both plays there is a conflation of lust with love, the appeal and resentment of what ones desires. Strindberg wrote *Miss Julie* for his wife, the aristocratic Siri von Essen. Their subsequent divorce was devastating to the playwright and left him convinced that women, not just his wife, but all women, were in a conspiracy to suck power from men. In *Streetcar* Stanley Kowalski is convinced his wife is being talked into just such a conspiracy by her sister Blanche.

A technical aspect of Strindberg's writing that echoes in Williams' craft is melodious speech erupting into tumultuous argument. In Strindberg's dialogue the sing-song of a Scandinavian language entices listeners to recognize disagreements between a man and a woman as music. Williams' mastery of the sound of spoken English—and the sounds of stage action—adds a similar beauty to many of his plays, among them *Streetcar* in which the lilt of flirtation gives way to shouts and moans. The slap of cards on the poker table has its own music.

Figures from Strindberg appear as well in *The Day on Which a Man Dies*—written by Williams between 1957 and 1960—in particular a vampire of a woman who, while her man sleeps, celebrates her victory with a dance: *"Her body is triumphantly alive: it proclaims how she took the man in the night and mastered his nerve-shattered body."*

In *Day on Which,* the rhythm and musicality of argument swells, engorged with rage. What passages of lyricism there are are usually wordless. The action in the text is a lover's quarrel. The main characters are The Man, an acclaimed painter now mocked for his new technique of applying paint with spray-guns; The Woman, the painter's sharp-tongued companion for eleven years, who has lost faith in him and lost faith in his work. The man and woman argue violently, make up, make love, and betray each other. The Man is based loosely on Jackson Pollock, whom Williams had known from Provincetown since 1940.

Strindberg and Williams both painted, in watercolor and in oil. Strindberg's use of paint, laid on with a trowel was—in process and resultant image—evocative of the turbulent sea. Williams' painting, more modest, nevertheless demonstrates his urge to express himself visually, as does his lifelong doodling. Both men wrote and made pictures, in part, to share what they saw in their waking dreams.

Williams' vision differs importantly from Strindberg's in its emphasis and insistence on the value of temporary peace, momentary rest, and short-lived love. The images given to express these respites vary, sometimes spoken, sometimes shown on stage or described in stage directions: a lit match, breakable glass, a bed in a hotel, a bird in flight. Their transience makes them that much more cherished while they flame, fly, glisten, or offer refuge. Williams often ends his plays with bubbles just before they burst, so that inevitable collapse shadows the buoyancy an audience sees, hears, and feels.

As refuge from battle, time-out in the corner before the fight resumes, Williams offers his characters rented beds. These are often in a boardinghouse, a Depression-era institution where unrelated tenants shared a home. Despite the ambivalent pleasures of anonymity, living in a boardinghouse—sharing the dining table and the bathroom—apes the life of a family left behind.

Willful retreat to asylum (if need be, a madhouse) as a way to defy (though not defer) defeat and death, is the strategy of Williams' last play on Broadway, *Clothes for a Summer Hotel,* written in 1980, less than three years before Williams died. Stage directions in *Clothes* ask that the action be framed by the ruins of the North Carolina hospital where Zelda Fitzgerald was killed in a fire in 1948. Ghosts in the ruins perform a final meeting in 1939 between Zelda, institutionalized for mental illness, and her husband Scott Fitzgerald, now a Hollywood hack. Scott will die within the year. He has come to give Zelda the news that this might happen, and to present her with a ring to remember him by. She will receive neither news nor ring. She returns in her mind to 1924 and the hotel on the French Riviera where she had an affair.

> Scott asks,
> *"Zelda, do you often hallucinate like this?"*
> To which she replies,
> *"Often as possible, Scott."*

The shards and fragments of the Fitzgerald's spent glamour intrude like splinters, sometimes painfully so, on their lives and in their memories. The couple who epitomized the roaring '20s are, by the late '30s, as ruined as their burnt out surroundings—mad, broke, angry, inappropriately dressed, and, worst of all, no longer young.

Williams' well-known *Sweet Bird of Youth* is a popularization of these ideas for a mass market. Best known to mainstream audiences through the 1962 film starring Paul Newman and Geraldine Page, the action begins in a hotel room where a Hollywood star and a hometown boy have run away together—to escape their different pasts. As in *Day on Which*, the pair argue violently, make up, make love, and betray each other. The woman explains: *"When monster meets monster, one monster has to give way…"* Waiting for both monsters, the common opponent that will knock them both out is the enemy, time—the title Williams gave for the one-act version of *Sweet Bird*. Stage directions for *The Enemy: Time* ask that the house (not the hotel) in which the scene is set be skeletal, made of shards and fragments, and that lamentations fill the air. In the full-length play the hometown boy is ruined by castration, in the movie by having his nose broken. The woman escapes in a soap bubble of hope but Williams, in a stage direction, makes it clear she is "equally doomed…We return to the huddling together of the lost, but not with sentiment, which is false, but with whatever is truthful in the moments when people share doom, when they face firing squads together."

At the urging of its director Elia Kazan, who read the early drafts, *Sweet Bird* echoed the personal struggles of its characters with a political battle—resonant of race riots in the film directed by Richard Brooks—though camouflaged as the suppression of personal scandal.

For Williams, the war for life, disguised or not, is constant. Out of that struggle, grace may come, scars turn to badges of honor, pain turns to glory, endurance to beauty. Time's corruption of the physical might be the only end, but memory (and live performance) celebrates struggle as the spirit's salvation. Blanche, for all her trembling, is a tiger, says Stanley, and he would know. And sometimes she trembles, not in fear, but in eager anticipation of the fight.

The Enemy: Time, *Gremlin Theatre, St. Paul, Minnesota, Peter Christian Hansen as Phil Beam, directed by Jef Hall-Flavin. TW Fest 2009. Photo courtesy of Gremlin Theatre.*

2010

Under the Influence

You make a stage for a performance the same way you make an altar: by setting space aside. You can raise a platform—the better to see what is put upon it; you can chalk a circle on the street, so that distance frames the action; you can raise the audience on balconies, so they look down on what happens below. Any way you make a stage, you divide from out of the public's space another space where something special happens on the area set aside: the performance. If it's an altar you're making, you set apart space to house the spirit of the divine.

In Clarksdale, Mississippi, where Tennessee Williams' family moved when he was six, they now perform his plays on family porches as part of the Mississippi Delta Festival. The audience brings folding chairs and sits on the lawns within eavesdropping distance. They have been doing this in Clarksdale since 1993. The impulse to gossip often lies behind our pleasure at the theater. Attending the "porch plays" has the advantage that what we

Orpheus Descending, *The Infinite Theatre, New York, Lucius Bryant III as The Conjure Man, directed by Nick Potenzieri. TW Fest 2011. Photo by Josh Andrus.*

might pass on the street and talk about furtively, we can, sitting on the lawn, openly savor and applaud.

Williams, remembering the front porch of his family's Clarksdale house (on which his grandmother kept a barrel of honey)—and remembering the verandas of New Orleans—set several plays on porches. Among others, there's that hot Delta porch in *27 Wagons Full of Cotton*, where we spy on the ticklish nuances of the good neighbor policy. In front of the French Quarter cottage of *Auto-da-Fé* a man exclaims "You rock on the porch and talk about clean white curtains. While I'm all flame, all burning!" Amanda, the mother of *The Glass Menagerie,* laments that her family's fire escape in St. Louis is a poor excuse for their porch back home. In *The Night of the Iguana*, there's a Mexican veranda—underneath that tropical porch a scaly thing scratches for its life.

In Williams' unfinished short play *American Gothic*, there's the front porch of the Midwestern farmhouse we don't quite see in the famous painting by Grant Wood. It's just behind the thin-lipped couple in the painting, and was a prominent part of the real Iowa farmhouse Grant Wood depicted. The play was written, his old friend William Jay Smith tells us, when Williams, still called Tom, was at the University of Iowa and Grant Wood was on the faculty there. Williams imagined, as most people do, that the unsmiling pair facing us are husband and wife. The young playwright gave these icons the back-story that their farm's withered crop is their son, not their corn.

Given the conventions of realistic theater when watching the porch plays, we can peer into the inner lives of the characters, of what's "private" on the stage: learning in *27 Wagons Full of Cotton*, that the chubby giggling girl is willingly seduced; in *American Gothic*, that the thin-lipped woman is repressing something, perhaps a scream. If we are moved by what Williams wrote, in our hearts we are moved across the border dividing the world of the audience from the world of performance. From where our bodies sit or stand to hear and see (and gossip), we are moved into the other world, the world of the spirit. This is the meaning of ecstasy, the ancient Greek ecstasis: ecs, ex, *out of* stasis.

"*The Diving Bell,*" a poem Williams wrote in the years between *The Glass Menagerie* and *A Streetcar Named Desire,* begins

> I want to go under the sea in a diving-bell
> And return to the surface with ominous wonders to tell.

It's the return that's important. Living our lives, we visit the theater and go home. To remain on the other side, the world of the spirit, is to escape: into death, sometimes, or madness, or some other release from physical circumstances. Early on in his career, Williams, wrote about such escapes. Those one-way trips are off stage. What's on stage are the confused people left behind. In the short early play *Summer at the Lake*, a domineering mother, ambitious for her son's future, listens to the sounds of him swimming—to where? In an early short play called *Escape* we eye a bunkhouse of convicts, tense black men straining to catch the sounds of a runaway prisoner chased by a pack of baying hounds. In these plays the other side is separated from what we see by water and a barbed wire penitentiary fence—but it might be reached by steady swimming or desperate crawling.

Both these "escape plays" sketch characters and events that reappear in Williams' later longer work, in which escapes are followed by returns. The son who ran off to sea with the merchant marines comes home to his domineering mother in *The Glass Menagerie*, in his memories, standing on stage, set apart by a spotlight.

In *Orpheus Descending*, as in *Escape*, a fugitive from a chain gang is heard, pursued by hounds, in the distance out the window of a Delta dry goods store. "Run fast, brother! If they catch you, you never will run again!" shouts Valentine Xavier, a roving guitar-player, central figure of *Orpheus*, who knows firsthand about chain gangs. Later in the play, it's Val who is urged to flee, but he does not run away.

In *Orpheus Descending,* Williams took on subject matter—a trip to hell and back— that preoccupied him for five decades. The first version, titled *Battle of Angels,* reordered the New Testament images he learned from his grandfather, an Episcopalian minister. In the grandson's play, the love of Christ turns fleshy when the Sheriff's wife paints a portrait of the Savior in the all-too handsome likeness of Val Xavier. Her rival for Val's love, according to the prompt book archived in Austin, Texas, "smashes the canvas stretcher over her knee and stuffs the picture into the stove's red belly" scandalizing the 1940 opening night audience in Boston. When a narrow-minded mob arrives with torches, Val is burned alive along with two women, one of whom rejoices, "to be free of the flesh that confused our purpose."

The next week, Boston censors demanded cuts and the rest of *Battle of Angels' run*, intended for Broadway that season, was canceled. In the first rewrite, a few months after Boston, an epilogue displays Val's scorched snakeskin jacket as a relic in a museum: returned from hell as history.

More rewrites manifested over the next seventeen years. The myth of Orpheus refocused Williams' imperative that we visit the other side—the hell of memory, sometimes—in order to regain lost love. Critics who couldn't see more, belittled *Orpheus Descending* as melodrama. The Broadway production ran a disappointing two months. Soon after its close, Williams began visiting a Freudian analyst, who suggested a respite from writing. Instead, the playwright began retelling the Orpheus myth in a new play about a willfully self-destructive poet.

This new play, *Suddenly Last Summer*, was rooted in Williams' idolization of Hart Crane—for a while the author in Tennessee's "only library, and all of it." Soon after college, Williams wandered America from the mountains of New Mexico to the beaches of Florida, dropping all other books along the way except for Hart Crane's *Collected Poems*. Crane's life—he was gay, with a mother as imperious as Tennessee's or Tom Wingfield's—and Crane's death—he jumped from a steamer into the Gulf of Mexico—reinforced Williams' personal myth that "perhaps it is only through self-immolation of such a nature that we living beings can offer to you the entire truth of ourselves within the reasonable boundaries of a book." Suicide, understood this way by a writer, is a step toward resurrection. In *Suddenly Last Summer*, the poet Sebastian Venable publishes one book a year, composed of one poem, until the summer Sebastian passes away and his death becomes that year's poem.

The recitation of Sebastian's "last poem" takes place inside the sweaty greenhouse of a mansion in the Garden District of New Orleans. It is said that this savage, hissing otherworld built in the heart of Southern gentility is based on a similar room in the Bultman House in New Orleans. Williams knew the Bultmans—

their Garden District mansion was connected by an inner door to the funeral home they owned—but additional inspiration for that garden room is Raymond Chandler's 1939 novel, *The Big Sleep*, and its 1946 film version. Chandler's description of an orchid hothouse, the humidified nest of a paralyzed parent in a wheelchair, stuck amid plants "with nasty meaty leaves and stalks like the fingers of dead men," foreshadows Williams' stage directions for *Suddenly Last Summer*'s "fantastic garden which is more a tropical jungle or forest" with "massive tree-flowers that suggest organs of a body, torn out, still glistening with undried blood."

Filmgoing was a lifelong pleasure for Williams, and he often wrote of the sanctuary offered by dimly lit movie theaters. A character in *Talk to Me Like the Rain and Let Me Listen*…rhapsodizes:

> I will sit in the back row with all that darkness around me and figures sitting motionless on each side not conscious of me. Watching the screen. Imaginary people. People in stories.

Such dreams annoy *The Glass Menagerie*'s Tom, who complains, "People go to the movies instead of moving!"

But it's at the movies while watching newsreels that both Toms—Wingfield and Williams—learned something of the world outside America, the war in Europe. Newsreels could also, on occasion, offer a view to the majority of Americans of that great "other" side of the United States, the world of African-Americans, separated by a color line of law and prejudice from the lives of white Americans. Newsreels, for example, about the "Scottsboro boys," brought awareness of nine black men falsely accused of rape in 1931 to the public (waiting to see the main feature at a movie theater), even for those who didn't or wouldn't read newspapers and preferred to sit in the dark.

From childhood on, Williams looked across a color line. In Clarksdale the railroad tracks divided the part of town where he lived with his grandparents from the neighborhood called "New World," where the black people lived. In college, he and his friend poet William Jay Smith, would travel across the Mississippi River from St. Louis, Missouri to the black ghettos of East St. Louis, Illinois, where Williams learned enough to set a play in an East Saint Louis brothel.

Williams rarely put the private lives of black people on stage. *Escape* is an anomaly. Sparked by the 1931 Scottsboro case, Williams wrote a short story, "Big Black: A Mississippi Idyll," that won honorable mention in a University of Missouri short story contest that same year. It was easier to include black characters (and homosexual men) and expect acceptance in fiction than it was in drama. *Escape*, a dramatic one-act variation of "Big Black," was written around 1939 and went unpublished and unperformed until 2005.

Although the color line was frequently bridged by music, black musicians stayed on one side of it when they stopped playing. Thanks to Jim Crow laws, piano virtuoso Fats Waller and guitarist Leadbelly couldn't eat with white people in Mississippi, but they could play for them in clubs and be heard on the radio or juke-boxes. The guitar Val carries in *Orpheus Descending* bears the signatures of a black pantheon: the cornet player King Oliver, Leadbelly, and the "Empress of the Blues" Bessie Smith. Williams' hometown of Clarksdale provided imagery as mythic for Williams as Orpheus.

> VAL: The name Bessie Smith is written in the stars!—Jim Crow killed her, John Barleycorn and Jim Crow killed Bessie Smith. She bled to death after an auto accident, because they wouldn't take her into a white hospital….See this name here? That's another immortal!
>
> LADY: Fats Waller? Is his name written in the stars, too?
>
> VAL: Yes, his name is written in the stars, too.

In the Mississippi Delta, Val, who is a Cajun from a bayou, ends up lynched, as if he were black. The witness to that lynching is the ancient, blue-black Conjure Man whose skin is "daubed with cryptic signs." His "Choctaw cry" is as much a sound from hell as the scuttling of an iguana under a veranda. The Conjure Man brandishes a bird's collarbone, noisy amulets, and unknown powders: all paraphernalia for visiting the dead.

The African-American community had many rituals for visiting the other side and returning, among them the jazz funeral, with a brassy march trudging to the cemetery and a brassier joyous dance-line parading through the streets, making a spectacle of the return from the grave. Among former slaves, happiness at death, in part, celebrated a belief that the spirits of the dead were reunited with their ancestors in Africa.

Jazz swung over into white America as popular music. Listening to jazz was downtime relaxation for Williams, especially in the small clubs of New Orleans, New York, and oddly, enough. Provincetown. The summer of 1947, his last summer on the Cape, Williams attended, repeatedly, the Atlantic House concerts of Miss Stella Brooks, known to *cognoscenti* as "the white Billie Holiday." A Dixieland band backed her tart voice on stage, while her off stage wit gained her famous friends, including Marlon Brando and Williams, who was finishing up the script for *A Streetcar Named Desire*. Could that famous cry of "Stella!" be an echo of Miss Brook's curtain calls at the A-House?

Seven years earlier in Provincetown, Williams took a break from writing to go down an alley to a theater at the edge of the Cape Cod Bay. A summer stock company was performing Eugene O'Neill's *Diff'rent* (1920) based on Provincetown gossip about a prissy young girl who turned into a faded flapper. Williams, in a 1936 college paper about O'Neill, admired the acknowledged master begrudgingly, quoting him only once:

> Suppose I was to tell you it's just Beauty that's calling me, the beauty of the far off and unknown, the mystery and spell of the East which lures me—the joy of wandering on and on—in quest of the secret which is hidden just over there, beyond the horizon?
> (Eugene O'Neill, *Beyond the Horizon*)

In *Diff'rent* the parlor of a New England townhouse serves the same dramatic function as a Delta front porch, and open sexuality is met with the same narrow-mindedness as it is in *Battle of Angels*.

What influenced Tennessee Williams as he wrote was a potent mix: his family homes, his grandfather's sermons, his university education, classical mythology, the blues, a jazz singer at the A-House, famous paintings, sensational news stories, a beloved poet, a rival playwright. All these are, all of them, tributaries to the otherworldly seas of his imagination.

Hart Crane, in a poem titled *"To the Cloud Juggler,"* calls out to the sun rising over the sea:

Wrap us and lift us, drop us then, returned
Like water, undestroyed, like mist, unburned…

Again, it's the return. The function of performers, priests, and visionary writers is to move between worlds on our behalf. This Williams did, voyaging far into the seas of imagination, returning with stories and descriptions and dialogue that heard aloud or read or enacted are the formula for us, too, to visit another world and return to our own.

Orpheus Descending, *The Infinite Theatre, New York, Irene Glezos as Lady, Thomas Beaudoin as Val Xavier, directed by Nick Potenzieri. TW Fest 2011. Photo by Josh Andrus.*

2011

Double Exposures

Waitress: Yes, Madam. The plat du jour is remnants of yesterday's.
—Tennessee Williams, *Now the Cats With Jewelled Claws*

In *Sunburst*, that diamond in the rough of a short play written by Tennessee Williams in 1980, a retired ("too-early") Broadway actress, marvelously named Sylvia Sails, puts her kidnappers to sleep by reciting Shakespeare. Tellingly it's a passage from Shakespeare's *The Tempest*, one of the last plays Shakespeare wrote, probably when he was in retirement, a play in which a magician renounces his powers. To gather her wits the besieged Miss Sails summons up a song by Shakespeare about time passing under the sea:

Miss Sails:—Memory test of lines, not for this occasion, or any occasion—just memory test…
"Full fathom five thy father lies.
Those are pearls that were his—"

—no, no…

The Besieging Wilderness, #2, photo by Clarence John Laughlin, 1937. Courtesy of The Clarence John Laughlin Archive at The Historic New Orleans Collection, acc. no. 1981.247.3.63.

"Of his bones are coral made.
Those are pearls that were his eyes"

Yes—clearing, without rest on three pillows…

"Nothing of him that doth fade
but—doth suffer a sea change
Into—into something rich and strange…"

Shakespeare's doubling of charnel house and treasure vault, where what fades also glimmers, is a layer, among others, that Tennessee Williams set down late in life—when he was very much not in retirement—as part of an accumulation of layers in his writing. Like the luster of a pearl or Japanese lacquer, they are meant to render a double-exposure of awareness that develops when memory overlaps immediate reality.

There is something about the state of Mississippi, where Williams was born a hundred years ago, that makes seeing double more likely. "It is easy to lead a double life in the Delta…" Williams wrote in the late story "Miss Coynte of Greene," "…in fact it is almost impossible not to." The great Mississippi author Eudora Welty thought so too, especially while chronicling the mythical town of Morgana, rendering the Delta landscape (and gossip) as a veil of words stretched over the world of ancient Greek myth, as Williams would do in *Orpheus Descending*. Each novel of

William Faulkner's mythical Yoknapatawpha County, Mississippi orchestrates a clash of recollections, histories, and descriptions in which contradictions pile on discordantly, rather than harmonize or cancel each other out, not unlike William's *Cat on a Hot Tin Roof*. In 1948, the photographer Clarence John Laughlin—based in New Orleans, Williams' second home—published a book of double-exposures titled *Ghosts Along the Mississippi*. These were not accidents of the camera, but deliberately artful (and, sometimes arch) double images, to which Laughlin gave titles as resonant as Williams' plays: "*The Apparition,*" "*The Mirror of Long Ago,*" "*A Memory of Undine,*" "*A Vision of Dead Desire.*" In "*Besieging Wilderness (No. 2)*" a pillared antebellum façade is embraced—or overrun—in double exposure with the limbs of vigorous trees (a motif from *A Streetcar Named Desire*: Blanche DuBois in Stanley Kowalski's arms). In the landscape of the defeated Confederacy the ruins of The War (pronounced sometimes so that it sounds to Yankee ears as The Woe) are always there, like bruises.

Williams—composing his plays, short stories, essays and poems—added a vision of the future to the double-exposure of past-and-present, sometimes prompted, as with Miss Sails' song from *The Tempest*, by thinking of the sea with its limitless expanse an image of eternity traced by past and passing waves. From the 1940s to the 1980s, the ocean often surfaced in Williams writing—as reflector, amplifier, cornucopia of inspiration, the sound of annihilating eternity ("Boom!" in *The Milk Train Doesn't Stop Here*

Anymore), and on occasion, the catch-all of a person's life. As he grew older, he chose to live near the ocean—in Key West—as he had lived near the ocean when he was young in Malibu, California; Saint Augustine, Florida; and Provincetown.

When Williams first arrived in Provincetown in 1940 he took note, as does anyone who pays attention there, that as the seas shift, so do the dunes and the colors of the sky. For Williams, in the late 1970s, thinking back thirty years to when he first came to the Cape, the place became a site (pun intended) where past, present, and future merged.

"Life is all—it's just one time. It finally seems to all occur at one time," he wrote in *Something Cloudy, Something Clear*, his 1981 play that binds the loves of his life to images just as memorably impermanent: the streak of a comet over Race Point as a lingering August sunset falls on the sometimes cloudy, sometimes clear memories of long gone faces. Almost ten years before, in 1972, working on his *Memoirs* his story shifts, often without warning to readers, between Williams at the moment of writing his book and the times in his past that he's writing about. His short story "Miss Coynte of Greene," also written in 1972, swings freely without explanation from the present to the past and back. As with Clarence John Laughlin's double exposures, the blurring in Tennessee Williams' memoir, plays, and stories is deliberate—though demeaned by short-sighted contemporary critics who claimed Williams had lost control of his craft, ignoring that Williams—like Welty, or Faulkner, or Laughlin—worked with juxtaposition rather than definition to release what was inherent in individual images or stories, but not apparent until images or stories were combined.

That the past and the present and the future might gain the significance of a design when related to each other was an idea that fascinated Williams even when he was young. *The Parade*, the first play he set in the Provincetown dunes, begun in 1940, takes for its title Williams' playwright's instinct that a procession—of time or love or anything—gains dramatic suspense when its conclusion is unknown.

> I am looking back at everything. I remember single days, hours. None of them was ever complete in itself. They were all expectant. You know what I mean? They had their faces all turned one way, toward the future.

By 1957, when he was revisiting *Battle of Angels*, another play he wrote at the Cape in 1940, (and there's a draft fragment of it quoted in *Something Cloudy, Something Clear*), Williams reflected further on the future in an essay that became his introduction to *Orpheus Descending*:

So much for the past and present. The future is called "perhaps," which is the only possible thing to call the future. And the important thing is not to allow that to scare you.

Fearless acceptance of the future—that the one thing we know is that it's unknowable—flies in the face of Amanda's warning to her son Tom in *The Glass Menagerie*:

> …the future becomes the present, the present the past, and the past turns into everlasting regret if you don't plan for it!

What Williams planned is that the action in his plays would fly in performance between what happened before what we see on stage and what we understand will happen after. The bridegroom grunt on leave in *Green Eyes* is haunted by the fighting he's left behind in "Waakow" (a stand-in for Viet Nam), when his honeymoon is over he'll return to fighting there. The futility of Alma's love for John in the body of *Summer and Smoke* is shadowed in the play's prologue by her childhood friendship with John as the boy next door, and framed in the play's epilogue by her future relations with the newest john in town.

A hotel room, the setting of so many plays by Williams, gives shape to the same idea that in living our lives—circling round a bed as in *Sunburst*, *Green Eyes*, or *The Traveling Companion*—we arrive from somewhere else, and eventually move on to a vast somewhere other, just as the tourists do en route to the Grand Canyon in Williams' early short play *Once In a Lifetime*.

Now the Cats with Jewelled Claws takes place in a different sort of way station, a restaurant in Times Square, where premonitions of disaster shadow lunch. Before the Apocalypse the daily special is a hash of yesterday's scraps, served, if ordered, by a waitress who embodies one of Williams wittier images of simultaneity: she's pregnant (the future), she has a never-explained black-eye (the past), and she's certainly present, if dim. And, as she tells her ominous maître d', when her shift is done, she's never coming back.

The impossibility of ever going backward is also announced by the not-so-subtly autobiographical "famous writer" from *The Traveling Companion*, a play written late in Williams' life:

VIEUX:…—where would I go back to? To me as difficult as reversing the way the earth turns…

In *The Two-Character Play* "There's no turning back on the road even if the road's backward" a brother says to his sister, evoking lives without a future, where the present relates only to the past. A brother and sister, both actors, are stranded on tour in a cold, abandoned theater. To keep themselves warm they rehearse a play, written by the brother, about a brother and a sister. Paralyzed by fear—in their lives and in the play within the play—the two are unable to leave the imaginary house they "live" in on stage, and unable to exit the theater they perform in, though outside their "real" door imaginary sunflowers rise, an invitation to come out into the radiantly real gold light.

More radiant images compacting past, present, and future—like the song from Shakespeare's *Tempest*—bejewel William's late writing as exhortations to move forward—En avant!, as his personal motto announced. Tempting fantasies of the future extending in front of the present energize Williams' late comic short stories: the onrushing train of *The Killer Chicken and the Closet Queen* headed for the Golden Shores; and the observation of Miss Coynte of Greene, in the story of the same name, that her pregnant mixed-race love-child, Michelle Moon, is carrying on family tradition.

> Miss Coynte put on her far-sighted glasses, the lenses of which were almost telescopic, and she then observed that Michele Moon, despite her condition, had engaged the young colored gatekeeper in shameless sexual play behind the family crypt of a former governor.
>
> Miss Coynte smiled approvingly.

Taking out our own far-sighted glass a hundred years after the birth of Tennessee Williams, twenty-eight years after his death, we don't quite get a focused long view. Nor should we expect one. In 1642, twenty-five years after the death of Shakespeare, the theaters where his plays might have been performed were closed—all over England—by the same Puritans who founded America. They stayed closed for eighteen years. By 1664, a hundred years after Shakespeare's birth, the Puritans had lost control over England, theaters were open again, but the consensus among critics was that while Shakespeare's works had some very pretty passages, the plays themselves were poorly constructed. Unencumbered by copyright laws, the Poet Laureate Nahum Tate tacked a happy ending onto the tragedy of *King Lear* calling the original, in an ironic echo of *The Tempest*, "a heap of jewels, unstrung and unpolish't; yet so dazzling in their disorder, that I soon perceiv'd I had seiz'd a treasure." It took another hundred years for David Garrick to establish Shakespeare as a writer with the playwright's own rules, and unique excellencies. Might it happen to Williams? Echoing his introduction to *Orpheus* back at him:

> The future is called "perhaps," which is the only possible thing to call the future.

2012

The Paradise Across the Alley: Tennessee Williams and Music

Her Father's Records, *Detail of a white-line woodcut by Bill Evaul, 2012.*

For what is the heart but a sort of—a sort of—instrument—that translates noise *into* music, *chaos into—*order…
—Tennessee Williams, *Camino Real*

Music in the plays of Tennessee Williams spills on stage from the paradise across the street: the happiness and grace that others enjoy, overheard by those in very different circumstances than grace or happiness. But if music is sometimes counterpoint to action, behavior, or setting in a Williams play, at the same time music inspires those who hear it—those of us in the audience as well as Williams' characters on stage—moving us to believe that just outside the window or just around the corner, paradise might be found—and the harmony of love.

Until he was seven, when his family moved to St. Louis, Williams lived in insular Mississippi towns where, in the years

before the first World War, to hear music played was an occasion to be sought out: a hymn in church on Sunday, a concert in the park on the Fourth of July. Carolers came out at Christmas; songs were sung at birthday parties and on New Year's Eve. Clarksdale, Mississippi, where Williams lived in his grandfather's rectory, is known to be the birthplace of the Mississippi blues, the songs of lamentation written and sung by black people accompanied by the throb of a guitar. To hear the blues, in the days before such things were recorded, a white man or woman crossed to the other side of town. In the Delta, black people, for safety's sake, didn't play where they weren't invited. In time, the blues, or jazz, or pop songs, or hymns could be listened to in any part of town by turning the dial on a radio or cranking up a gramophone.

In New Orleans, every day's a holiday: races and music mix together, particularly in the French Quarter, where Williams moved in 1939. In the Quarter, a distinction of staid affluence is to live in relative silence, music arrives uninvited: marching bands block the crosswalks; a lonesome piano calls from the back of an alley; rowdy parties in the Bourbon Street joints echo down the narrow streets of the Vieux Carré. Among the poor, and Williams was poor when he first lived in the Quarter, the ubiquity of the radio blaring the peppy propaganda of "happy songs" during the Depression years was an innately theatrical irony begging to be placed in short stories or on stage.

When Williams declared his ambition to create a "plastic theatre," by plastic he meant a scientific term, the pliant, elastic response of a form to force, something he had heard discussed by the abstract expressionist Hans Hofmann and the great German theater director Ervin Piscator. Williams' plastic theater is a molten arena of restless forces. As Amanda recalls her gentlemen callers, the romantic music and her ecstatic voice rise to meet the deflating irony of words projected on a screen. Williams took Piscator's idea that music itself was a force, altering the significance of behavior and text, it didn't always need to parallel what the actors did or felt or said. Music wasn't necessarily sad when the characters were sad, as music would be to set the mood in a melodrama or a silent film. For Williams, it's a girl with a limp who hears dance hall tunes; it's a buttoned-up matriarch (from *Auto-da-Fé*) who is assaulted by "the idiotic gaiety" of "juke organs," it's jailbirds sadistically roasted to death in prison who hear the saccharine "I'm Forever Blowing Bubbles." The audience, not someone in the play, makes sense of the mix; sometimes characters refuse to mix. In *Streetcar*, for example, Stanley throws a radio out the window rather than hear that distracting rumba Blanche plays during his poker game from the other side of the makeshift curtain.

Like the rumba on the other side of the curtain, music overheard in a play by Williams hints at an alternate reality—often associated with the color blue: the blue piano (not the blues piano) of *Streetcar*, the blue guitar of *Camino Real*. The blue of the music is meaningful in the same way that Williams assigned meaning to blue light and blue costumes as the color of night and, sometimes, madness. The reverberations of blue and blue music are set out in a poem written by Wallace Stevens in 1937 "The Man with the Blue Guitar"—also the title of Stevens' fourth book of poems, and a character in Williams' play *Ten Blocks on the Camino Real*.

They said, "You have a blue guitar, You do not play things as they are."

> The man replied, "Things as they are
> Are changed upon the blue guitar."
>
> [And they said then, "But play, you must,
> A tune beyond us, yet ourselves,
>
> A tune upon the blue guitar
> Of things exactly as they are."]
> (from *The Man with the Blue Guitar* by Wallace Stevens)

In Mexico and Italy, Williams soaked up the music played by street musicians and he put that music, too, into his plays. Celebratory or mournful, the Spanish and Italian songs in Williams' plays reveal the emotion, often unspoken, of an on stage scene, avoiding competition with the words understood by the English-speaking audience. In *Talk to Me Like the Rain and Let Me Listen*, someone in the neighborhood of tenements practicing chords from the Mexican ballad "Estrellita" betrays the unmentioned tenderness between a bickering, young couple. In *Sweet Bird of Youth* the heart-on-the-sleeve canción *Quiereme Mucho* floods a loveless cocktail lounge. The third block of ten on the Camino Real begins with this:

[*There is a fading of light. First dusk falls on the plaza with an effect of coolness. At some distance a woman begins to sing.*]

Noche de ronda,	/	Night sentry
Que triste pase,	/	How sadly you pass
Que triste cruza	/	How sadly you cross
Por mi balcon!	/	By my balcony!

[*The guitar player steps suddenly forward and sweeps his strings.*]

(from *Ten Blocks on the Camino Real*)

The guitar is the musical instrument we hear and see most often in a Tennessee Williams play. Practical on stage: portable, affordable, and it's relatively easy to teach an actor to play one. Versatile, too, the guitar can carry the tunes and essence of *canciónes,* Italian folk songs, the blues, 1930s country-western, and its 1950s descendant rock and roll. In *Orpheus Descending* a guitar is the totem of the messianic blues player, in *The Traveling Companion* it's a hardened street hustler's soft spot, in early versions of *The Rose Tattoo* a guitar heard outside a shuttered window makes a tough young widow weep. In *Kingdom of Earth,* it surprises us when a guitar gets swung off a hook to enter as an instrument of flirtation and menace.

A phonograph has its own meaning in a play by Williams. Phonograph music is often a way to retreat into the past, often an unwanted or unappreciated legacy:

…those worn-out phonograph records your father left as a painful reminder of him?

(from *The Glass Menagerie*)

Orchestras and harpsichords arrive on stage via phonographs: Tchaikovsky's "None But the Lonely Hearts" in *Portrait of a Madonna,* Landowska's Bach sessions in *Something Unspoken,* Maurice Ravel's "Pavane for a Dead Princess" in *Something Cloudy, Something Clear*—all of these halo what's ephemeral on stage with a sense of eternal importance by a connection to classical form. Music from recordings can also signal impermanence, as happens during the flashbacks to murder and suicide in *Suddenly Last Summer* and *Streetcar,* and during the on stage suicide in *The Day on Which a Man Dies.*

Music was important enough to Williams in his personal life that, with the first real money he had (from a Rockefeller Grant), he bought himself a wind-up Victrola with a silver horn and toted it to Provincetown and later to Nantucket. We know the thick vinyl 78s he played on it: Caruso arias, that "Pavane" by Ravel, a lot of schmaltz: "The Santiago Waltz," "The Golondrina," and memorably, Bing Crosby's version of "Sweet Leilani." These recordings would resound in his plays for the next five decades: "La Golondrina" in five plays, "Estrellita" in at least three. "I'm Forever Blowing Bubbles" pops up in at least three plays.

In the original Broadway productions of Williams' plays, music clued the audience to the tone of the writing, which we forget was, in its time, so experimental as to be incomprehensible without help. Paul Bowles, a close friend of Williams for decades, provided music for the Broadway productions of five plays by Williams. Theater critics consistently praised the delicate beauty and strength of Bowles' music, even when they didn't like Williams' plays, but the Bowles scores do not much survive in recordings or written scores. One exception, the Bowles *Glass Menagerie* score. Listening to it we learn that for all the narrator's talk of "the fiddle in the wings," it's the harp Bowles added to underscore the shimmer of the spoken words that extends the narrator's distance in time from the story being told.

…in memory, everything seems to happen to music.
(from *The Glass Menagerie*)

In film adaptations of Williams' work, music swayed emotional response and understanding. Alex North's score for *Streetcar*, the first ever jazz score for a Hollywood film, is so powerful it stirred the censor to demand the honky-tonk hip-swaying music for Stella's return to her abusive husband be replaced by some accompaniment less blatantly lewd. To comply, in the version released by Warner Brothers, as Stella lurches down the spiral wrought iron stairs, an Aaron Copland-like fanfare trumpets family values. The Kenyon Hopkins score for *The Fugitive Kind* is disarmingly soft and brings out the softness of Marlon Brando's performance while setting a mesmerizing slow place that the director, Sidney Lumet, intended to help the audience ruminate on this otherworldly film adapted from *Orpheus Descending*. Elmer Bernstein's score for *Summer and Smoke* functions traditionally: an orchestra swells with emotion to indicate to the audience what is meant to be felt. Max Steiner's grand score for the first film of *The Glass Menagerie*, released in 1950, is part of the misguided fullness (Steiner wrote the score for *Gone With the Wind*) that brings to the audience's eyes and ears what Williams deliberately left unresolved in the play, including the addition of a scene where Laura crosses the street to the Paradise Dance Hall as her mother and brother look on and speak dreamily of her happiness.

In the plays, rather than the films, the crossing-over takes place in the audience, induced by what's on stage, and in particular induced by music. In the experimental *I Never Get Dressed Till After*

Dark on Sundays the on stage rehearsal process shows how that's done; music is played on cue so that the audience hears the blues woven into the sounds of a woman sobbing.

The choice of accompaniment is a matter of interpretation, of course, but what would lovemaking, brutal or tender, be without music in a play by Williams? As Kilroy explains to the gypsy's daughter:

> …that's the way we do things in the States. A little vino, some records on the Victrola, some quiet conversation—and then if both parties are in a mood for romance…[*Gesture.*]

Chorus Girls Photographic Essay

In 2013 Josh Andrus photographed *The Chorus Girl Plays* in Provincetown, a burlesque show framing three Depression-era plays by Williams in which chorus girls have major roles. Choreographed by Chicago's Paula Frasz for her own DanszLoop Chicago ensemble, under the direction of Berlin-based British director, Robert Chevara, the burlesque routines morphed directly into and out of the uninterrupted performance of the texts. Andrus, confronting the difficulty of shooting fast-moving dancers under lurid stage lighting, captured the burlesque show's confrontation with gravity. The dancers are giddy, earthy, exhausted, sometimes resplendent, sometimes befuddled, sometimes in control, always balancing themselves upright despite their circumstances.

Lefty Lucy, Miss Coney Island USA 2011, as the headliner for The Chorus Girl Dances *by DanszLoop Chicago, Chicago, IL choreographed by Paula Frasz for* The Chorus Girl Plays. *Background from left to right: Tarah Brown, Christina Eltvedt Margin, Katie Matteson Campana. TW Fest 2013. Photo by Josh Andrus.*

The Chorus Girl Dances by Dansz-Loop Chicago, Chicago, IL choreographed by Paula Frasz for The Chorus Girl Plays. *Pictured left to right: Tarah Brown and Katie Matteson Campana. Directed by Robert Chevara. TW Fest 2013. Photo by Josh Andrus*

The Chorus Girl Dances *by Dansz-Loop Chicago, Chicago, IL choreographed by Paula Frasz for* The Chorus Girl Plays. *Pictured left to right: Margaret Reynolds and Todd Rhoades. Directed by Robert Chevara. TW Fest 2013. Photo by Josh Andrus.*

The Chorus Girl Dances by DanszLoop Chicago, Chicago, IL choreographed by Paula Frasz for The Chorus Girl Plays. Foreground: Katie Matteson Campana. Background from left to right: Christina Eltvedt Margin, Margaret Reynolds, Todd Rhoades, Paul Christiano. Directed by Robert Chevara. TW Fest 2013. Photo by Josh Andrus.

At Liberty, *DanszLoop Chicago, Chicago, IL. Christina Eltvedt Margin as Bessie, Paula Frasz as the Mother, directed by Robert Chevara in* The Chorus Girl Plays. *TW Fest 2013. Josh Andrus.*

2013

Fifty Percent Illusion: Tennessee Williams and Women

"After all, a woman's charm is fifty percent illusion…"
—Blanche DuBois in *A Streetcar Named Desire*

Tennessee Williams celebrates illusion in all his plays, the making of illusion and the makers of illusion. Fortitude, beauty, and good lighting, are, in the eye of Williams, illusions all. That's not to say powerless, quite the opposite. Women, in particular, are mighty illusionists on the Williams stage, something more than magicians turning water into whiskey or canaries into goldfish, their act is to transform themselves. The more famous charmers—Amanda and her daughter Laura from *The Glass Menagerie*, Maggie the Cat on that hot tin roof, and of course, Blanche DuBois from *A Streetcar Named Desire*—are often so beguiling they appear to levitate, though each is tethered to earth by their creator's understanding of women, beginning with the

The Chorus Girl Dances *by Dansz-Loop Chicago, Chicago, IL choreographed by Paula Frasz for* The Chorus Girl Plays. *Pictured Katie Matteson Campana. Directed by Robert Chevara. TW Fest 2013. Photo by Josh Andrus.*

familiar secret sadnesses of his sister, his mother, and his grandmother. In creating women's roles, Williams understood that women—as Blanche points out in *Streetcar*—have had to create illusions for themselves (and for others) in order to survive.

Though Williams, born in 1911, and his women are for all time, they are also very much of their own time. The Great Depression formed their characters, Williams and his women, those less-than-great ten years after 1929 and before the World War started in Europe, a decade when women in America were often on their own financially and often self-sufficient emotionally.

What young Thomas Lanier Williams saw and heard projected in Depression-era films took him beyond personal experience, family secrets, and his own fantasies to Hollywood fantasies of show biz, set in the backstage world of Broadway musical comedies where wise-cracking, swell-looking dames not only survived, but prevailed. The girls in the chorus, whose figures and wits were a means to survive, became, it would seem, Williams' templates of a lady. The Ziegfeld Follies' statuesque beauties stepped down from their pedestals to parade in a line. Their descendants, the chorus girls of the thirties, lined up to kick their legs or, sometimes, stepped down to burlesque. Sometimes they stepped out on the wrong side of town to sell their acts in the street.

In Williams' earliest plays—before he was Tennessee, while he was still Tom—a chorus girl type reappears from play to play as if cast from a repertory company of Williams' imagination. In his first play, *Beauty is the Word* (1930), a chorus girl is in Pago Pago with her missionary aunt teaching the natives to dance on the beach. She's unhappily married to a starving New York artist in *The Magic Tower* (*1936*), and runs away to go back on tour where we later see her in *In Our Profession* (1938). She's Wanda, the ambitious girlfriend in *The Parade* (1940). In *At Liberty* (1941), the poor thing has tuberculosis and moves back home to Mississippi, where she still reads *Variety* in hopes of finding a job.

By definition, a chorus girl can be expected to dance, sing, dress up, and sooner or later undress. The most glamorous glamour puss is shown—in films of the day and in Williams' plays—backstage or home, taking off her finery or getting ready to go out, putting on the Ritz. If we see her in furs or feathers it's a good bet we'll eventually see her in her slip, not just to be titillating, though there is that, but for a further reveal: if a woman's charm is fifty percent illusion, the other half is the illusion-maker—the woman of her own appearance and, by analogy, the playwright of a play. Williams shows us women dressing and undressing in order to dramatize their power to enchant, and his own.

He shows us the power to deflate, too. In life, it's a lot of work, getting in and out of the girdle or stockings, flash-boiling that witty retort. Sooner or later it's time to take a break, conclude the show, go home, rest, take those heels off and put a corn plaster in place.

In *Cairo, Shanghai, Bombay!* (1935) Millie does just that,

> …when a young an' innocent gal like me ain' got no mother to guide her footsteps down that good ole straight an' narrow way.…Why the nex' bes' thing's a box of Blue Jay Corn-Plasters, Honey! Blue Jay f'r me! (She sighs contentedly as she places the plaster over her aching toe.)

For Williams, more profound relief is associated—always—with the ocean and the sound of waves. *Cairo, Shanghai, Bombay!* is true to formula. Two girls bring sailors home to the Bronx—a drab setting for the occluded dreams that punctuate the title, but even so those dreams flash.

> Aileen (sobbing hysterically): We was gonna do such wonderful things together, Millie. We was gonna buy us a little fifty feet schooner, he said, and sail all over the seas! We was gonna take turns at the wheel. His watch and my watch, Millie. We was gonna see the Southern Cross at night. Stars, Millie. Thousands and thousands of stars. And smell the sea. Feel the wind in our faces.

Fantasies of escape by sea resurface in other Williams plays early and late—Flossie, the gun moll in *Curtains for the Gentlemen* dreams of the beach in Miami as does Bessie in *At Liberty*, as will Blanche in *Streetcar*. Sailors, the men from the sea who go back to the sea, will wash up for a while in *The Mutilated*, in *The Milk Train Doesn't Stop Here Anymore*, and morph into the half-naked men—titillating, too, but something more—who enter wet or washing in *Kingdom of Earth* and *Cat on a Hot Tin Roof*. Anything watery: the rain, the dew—even the water from Brick's shower in *Cat* or the rising river in *Kingdom*—runs to the sea, and an abundance of water—flood, sea, or weeping—spills to annihilation. *Boom!* as the poet says when the *Milk Train* stops. Even the statue of General Andrew Jackson in *The Mutilated* "is all wet shiny green like he rode up out of the sea."

> I'll be buried at sea sewn up in a clean white sack and dropped overboard—at noon.
>
> (Blanche in *Streetcar*)

It's reflex to read the early plays by the light of the later classics, but reverse the process and new meanings appear. If the early plays have, to our eyes, unresolved endings, that is an opportunity to see their separate parts. Williams had not yet lived enough, suffered enough, succeeded enough, nor spent enough mornings at his typewriter to resolve these aspects, and so they lie exposed and easier for us to note: we meet a chorus girl in the city, but she comes from out in the sticks; strong in so many ways, her weakness is drink; as hard-boiled as she is, she pairs herself to a dreaming mate. The chorus girl offers sisterly pity for other women who are drowning, but she won't willingly go down with them, not into madness or down into the sea. She might, though, like the molls, in *American Gothic* and *Curtains for the Gentleman*—or Stella with Stanley, Maggie with Brick—follow her hellbent man where he intends to go.

> MARGARET: *Oh, Brick!* How long does it have t' go on? This punishment? Haven't I done time enough, haven't I served my term, can't I apply for a—pardon?

Williams saw that in a world dominated by men, women longed for the thing that would dominate, if not destroy, them. A psychoanalyst might diagnose sadomasochism, but to the poet, and Williams was that, those longings are submission to something larger than oneself, as large as an ocean or a God.

It's a partial view, to see Williams and his women in a sociological way, in a political way, as reflections of their time, or as projections of his own experience. The women in his plays are part of and contribute to an imaginary landscape of his own envisioning and their aspects were reconfigured as he found new and different ways to report on his vision—even as it changed. Which it did.

Williams lived long enough—until February 1983, when the Equal Rights Amendment was still being voted on among the states—to see the roles of women evolve in American society. Williams' strategies for creating women's roles changed as well. Though his women would always seek grace, there would be "no more southern belles" Williams said about his later work, heralding the hot-pink survivalist who climbs above the flood waters, Myrtle from *Kingdom of Earth*, and Trinket Dugan in *The Mutilated*, who gets down on her knees to pray with her conniving friend Celeste so they can both avoid Jack in Black (i.e. Death) for a little while.

Charging women with strength, not to mention sexual desire, in any of his plays, early or late, brought on the accusation that Williams had created unreal monsters. Fools claimed that Williams' women were really men in drag, like Michelangelo's sculptures of Night, male bodies with female appendages. If a strong woman is monstrous then the women of strength in Williams plays are unashamed to proclaim themselves monsters, as do the Princess in *Sweet Bird of Youth* and Sissy Goforth in *The Milk Train Doesn't Stop Here Anymore*.

Many of these strong women have chorus girl pasts. Sissy boasts of her life in the *Follies* (pretty good for a "Georgia swamp bitch," as she calls herself). Myrtle was formerly The Personality Kid and the Headless Girl (which was once a real sideshow act). The greatest day in mutilated Trinket Dugan's life was when she dressed up as a widow and lead a funeral parade for Mr. Depression under a steady rain. Notice how *Cat on a Hot Tin Roof* reverses the sexual roles and rules, beginning with Maggie's disdain:

> …a cotton carnival queen…well, that's one honor that I don't envy…Sit on a brass throne on a tacky float an' ride down Main Street, smilin', bowin', and blowin' kisses to all the trash on the street.

Cat has other switcheroos: it's Brick in his pajamas, not a chorus girl in her slip, who has the problems with liquor and a man that got away. Maggie, like other strong women, is bent on survival:

> …one thing I don't have is the charm of the defeated, my hat is still in the ring, and I am determined to win!

Win what? Williams' portraits of women were dismissed for decades by male critics who weren't quite sure what women or Williams wanted (or were). A bevy of women critics, though, none of them southern, recognized Williams' women as reality: Allean Hale (who passed away just shy of her 101th birthday in 2015, began intense research on Tennessee Williams in the early 1960s), Linda Dorff (who passed away in 2000 at the age of 49), Ruby Cohn (who passed away in 2011 at the age of 89), and Annette Saddik (who is alive and kicking). Liz Ashley, a famous interpreter of Maggie the Cat, recently said that when she was a child in Baton Rouge, what astonished her watching a performance of Williams' play *Summer and Smoke* was that people were up on stage talking about things and showing things that they never discussed in her family, or if so, in whispers.

Without whispering, Williams' women own up to their chorus girl pasts. Sissy and Myrtle and Maggie—like Flossie (*Curtains for the Gentleman*), Bessie (*At Liberty*), Millie and Aileen (*Cairo, Shanghai, Bombay!*)—are the makers of their own illusion and, like burlesque performers, they own and enjoy the power of their femininity. Nine months after Williams died, the Equal Rights Amendment failed to be ratified. To perform his plays now, and to watch them performed, is to continue a conversation about women's roles, illusory and real, on stage and off.

2014

Circle of Friends

In June of 1946, with *The Glass Menagerie* still playing on Broadway (since March of the year before), Tennessee Williams decided he and his lover, Pancho Rodriguez—they had been living together since February—would spend the summer in Nantucket. Williams rented a house at 31 Pine Street and invited Carson McCullers, with whom he had exchanged letters but had never met, to stay with them. She accepted.

Williams and McCullers worked that summer, sitting across from each other at a big table in the dining room. He was rewriting what became the fifth full-length play of his professional career, *Summer and Smoke;* unsatisfied with a version begun by someone else, she was adapting her third novel, *The Member of the Wedding,* into a play. There was a wind-up Victrola with a silver horn (that Williams carried to Provincetown in 1940), which spun out Sousa marches and the *Santiago Waltz*. The recordings, pompous and silly, evoke a small town orchestra playing in a gazebo. Williams inserted such an orchestra into his play.

Carson McCullers, July 31, 1959, photo by Carl Van Vechten, courtesy of Library of Congress, Prints & Photographs Division, Carl Van Vechten Collection (reproduction number, e.g., LC-USZ62-54231).

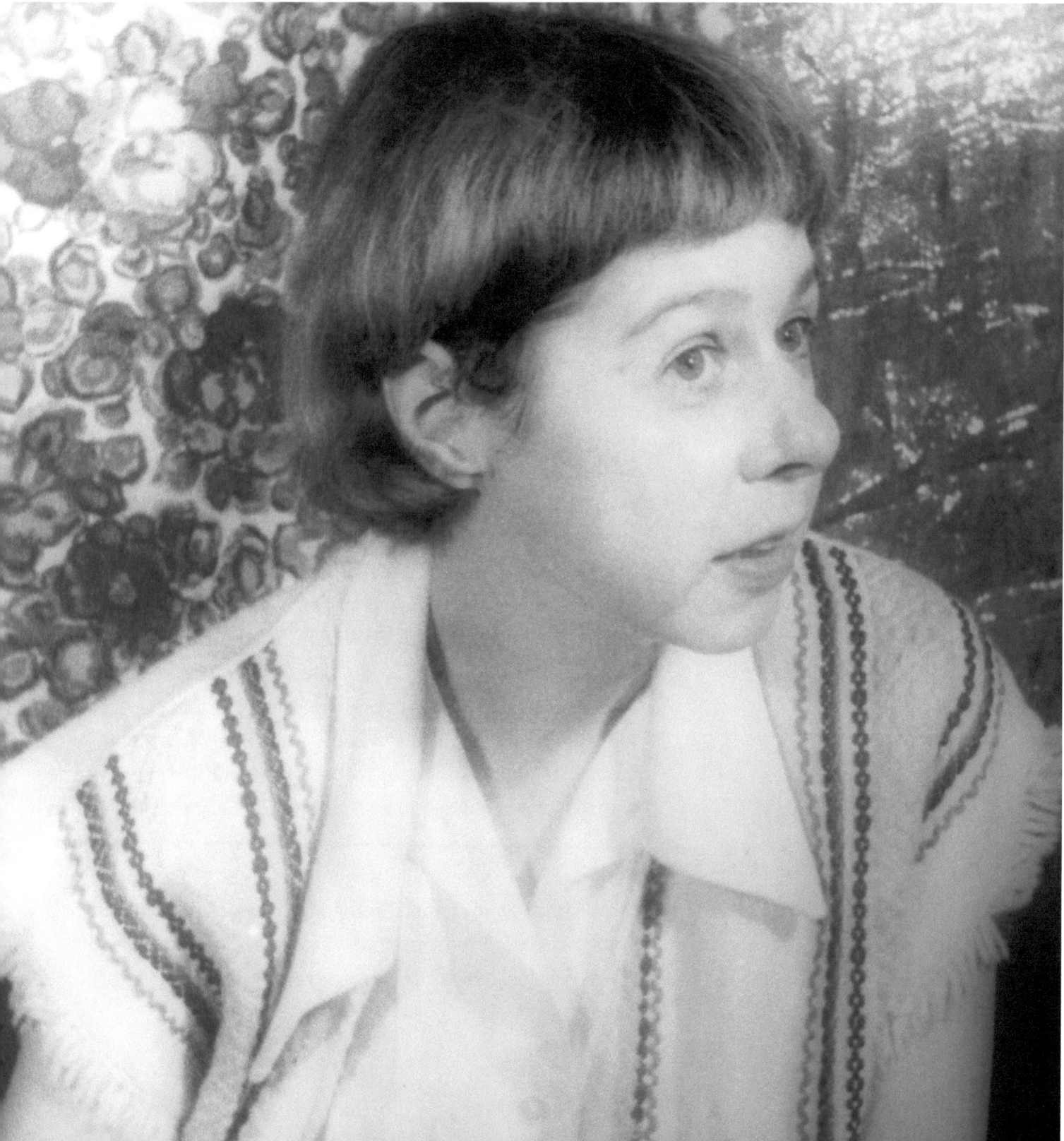

Southerners in New England, thinking of the South, they drank Johnny Walker during the day, hot rum with tea at night. Day and night they took walks along the beach, enjoying the sunsets and the Aurora Borealis, which was unusually bright that year. Carson was mooning over a woman who kept pigs. On a visit to Carson's would-be lover, Williams shared enough Johnny Walker with the pigs to get them drunk.

In his plays, Williams depicts writers who know each other socially as squabbling rivals, trading banter: Hemingway and Fitzgerald bicker in Williams' *Clothes for a Summer Hotel* and in *The Notebook of Trigorin,* (Williams' adaptation of Chekhov's *Seagull*) the short-story writers Treplev and Trigorin describe each other with withering dismissals. In Williams' life, catty remarks were tossed at him and thrown back to his friends Donald Windham, Gore Vidal, and Truman Capote, that is to say, other gay writers of his generation whose criticism Williams endured, even as he tolerated their work as playwrights (yet somehow passing on to them that he knew himself to be the superior dramatist—and was). No one could be quite so cutting to Williams as those men who knew enough to cut close and deep. Williams gave as good as he got. Gore Vidal, in an unintentionally self-revealing review of Williams' *Memoirs* titled "Some Memories of the Glorious Bird and an Earlier Self" cracked that "The Bird seldom reads a book," to which Williams replied, "He means I seldom read one of his."

Among writers Tennessee Williams considered his peers—Carson McCullers, Yukio Mishima, Jane Bowles, and William Inge, and some few others—there was mutual respect and not so much sniping, until Inge grew successful enough in the 1950s to eclipse Williams.

What we know of the lives of these writers Williams befriended and respected (as writers), brings to mind something essential about Williams and that circle of friends. They were in pain. McCullers contracted rheumatoid arthritis when she was fifteen. By the time she was thirty-one, a series of strokes left her paralyzed on the left side of her body. The hand with which she held her cane was curved like a hook and shivered involuntarily. Jane Bowles had trouble with her right knee, according to family legend, since the time in early childhood when she was dropped by her nurse. At fourteen, Jane fell from a horse, broke her right leg, endured four unsuccessful operations, developed tuberculosis of the knee that went undiagnosed, and spent two years in traction, all of this before she was seventeen.

Like McCullers, Bowles lived with constant pain and walked with a pronounced limp. Bowles suffered a massive stroke when she was forty, leaving her incapacitated until her death at fifty-six. Inge's mental illnesses could be just as debilitating. By the end of his life he recognized that the psychiatric treatments offered him had increased his agony. Mishima's defined abdominal muscles were impossible for him to develop without willfully self-imposed pain, something Mishima made into an aesthetic. Williams' childhood illnesses, eye surgeries performed without anesthesia, and varied agonizing adult ailments, from hemorrhoids to heart palpitations, were augmented by crippling depression and anguished panic attacks.

Along with pain, these friends shared a work ethic. McCullers, who dictated a memoir as she was dying, called it "the grace of hard work." Williams, from out of the depths of depression, managed to write every morning. Mishima's output is astounding. By the time of his death, at forty-five, he had completed thirty-four novels, over fifty plays, twenty-five books of short stories, and at least thirty-five books of essays. What Jane Bowles considered her finished output included much, much less: one novel, one full-length play, a ten-minute puppet play, and eleven stories. She worried over her words painfully, yet she was compelled to undergo the ordeal of writing as much as Mishima was compelled to undergo the rigors of bodybuilding.

Along with hard work, they drank hard, and they drank together when they could. They enjoyed themselves shamelessly, with the exception of Inge, whose accommodation with American middle-class respectability included Alcoholics Anonymous meetings, teaching in a high school, and visits to a well-meaning analyst, but for all that, Inge continued to break out of bounds, followed by bouts of hot shame. Williams, much less scrupulous, went to the same shrink, fell off the wagon in two weeks, and boasted about it in interviews.

Drinking fueled their shared aesthetic. Ecstasy is a higher value in their work than sobriety, even if ecstasy lasts a shorter time. An inevitable crash is the price, a cost they knew about intimately and, in living their lives, paid. Suicide was a possibility. Williams and McCullers tried, McCullers' father and her husband eventually succeeded, as did Williams. Mishima's suicide, ritual disembowelment, planned for months, is so in character with his writing it can be considered the last of his dramas. Inge's short play, *The Love Death,* written between 1968 and 1970 and published posthumously, begins with a failed writer tricking his psychiatrist to reveal the number of sleeping pills it takes to kill oneself, which the writer then swallows. In 1973, Inge asphyxiated himself inside his garage seated behind the wheel of his new Mercedes. Thinking of the roses that repeat in their titles or the names of their characters, roses that blossom and shatter, scattering petals, spurred by the Romantic impulse to give all and then fall exhausted, these writers understood sacrifice and martyrdom. Mishima was photographed as St. Sebastian (in a book titled *Ordeal of Roses*). In Williams' late play *Vieux Carré,* the dying painter Nightingale, before he's carried off on a stretcher, holds his easel "over his head like a crucifix to exorcise a demon."

The flip side of their pain is that they were successful, on their own terms and in the greater world. They were fashionable—and ambitious. They wanted their plays on Broadway, they wanted Hollywood films made out of what they wrote with Hollywood stars and important directors. In the 1950s they got what they wanted. They won awards. Mishima won many prizes in Japan and his Kabuki plays were performed at the preeminent Kabuki-za. Inge won a Pulitzer and an Oscar, Williams two Pulitzers. Carson McCullers' adaptation of *The Member of the Wedding* won the New York Drama Critics' Circle Award for best play in 1950. Williams won the same award four times, Inge won it, too. They were photographed by celebrity photographers, and there was interest enough about them for potential scandal.

They led secret lives sexually. In the 1950s Williams and Inge were closeted and sexually active. According to reliable sources, they had sex with each other. Bowles and McCullers and Mishima were married, but before and during their marriages, they had sex with members of their own sex. They were careful to keep their secrets secret—enough to avoid the law and maintain what was then considered good and a decent reputation.

After they died, some of their heirs maintained increasingly quaint façades, but those have collapsed with the weight of time. We know now some of the specifics of Bowles, McCullers, and Mishima in bed because their lovers have squealed. Williams, characteristically, spilled his own details in *Memoirs*.

Their sexual activity gave them ready metaphors for their writing: enslavement, abandon, weakness in wanting the thing that would destroy them and, especially and always, having a secret, knowing a secret, keeping a secret, sharing a secret. At an early age their unconventional behavior estranged them from conventional parents and peers. They identified with freaks because they knew what it was to be one. Bowles, who was born Jewish, called herself Crippie, the Kike Dyke. Mishima's father mocked him as effeminate, Williams' father called him Miss Nancy. Inge was called a sissy by the other boys in Independence, Kansas, and he was. Bowles and McCullers were "boyish." In each other's company they were open about who they slept with.

The society they chose to enter held freewheeling soirées in out of the way places: Tangiers, Key West, and the Brooklyn boardinghouse where Carson McCullers and Jane Bowles sometimes roomed (separately) with Gypsy Rose Lee and W.H. Auden. Carson had a crush on Gypsy, though Williams denied it was consummated. He was wrong.

Yet, for all that, they were lonely—profoundly lonely. They fell in love with inaccessible people, which seems fair because they were themselves inaccessible. Their vision made them so, they were not always in the room with other people but off somewhere else in their minds. They recognized this in each other's writing, and in each other's company. In reading each other, in knowing each other, I do not think they were any less lonely, but instead they were lonely together.

In *Camino Real*, Williams has Don Quixote say:

When so many are lonely as seem to be lonely, it would be inexcusably selfish to be lonely alone.

Being alone together is often if not always the basis of friendship in Williams' plays.

Alone together/together alone, in life, off-stage, Williams offered his friends adventures to share, often road trips. In early 1939 he hitched cross country from New Orleans to Malibu with the clarinet player Jim Parrott; he once proposed that Carson McCullers run off with him to set up a ranch in the West with his sister Rose. Plays by Williams in which friendship is a major theme inevitably suggest a rush out the door: to a picnic in *A Lovely Sunday for Creve Coeur,* to the Pacific Coast in *Vieux Carré,* to a ranch in Texas with photogenic cattle in *Period of Adjustment*. That traveling companions might arrive at contentment is possible, but unlikely. As with the lovers Williams imagined, friends in Williams' plays share fantasies: the starving ladies in *Vieux Carré* pretend to eat at fancy French Quarter restaurants, the suburban husbands in *Period of Adjustment* expect to become successful ranchers. Usually the women who are friends in Williams plays want to make homes together and squabble, as in *Creve Coeur*, *The Mutilated*, and *Something Unspoken*. There are exceptions: the chippies in *A Perfect Analysis Given by a Parrot* run off together and squabble.

At home or out the door, true friends are rare in plays by Williams. Lovers are more likely. Attempts to transfigure friends to lovers usually fail (*The Night of the Iguana* is the great exception) and are inevitably painful and embarrassing. In *Summer and Smoke*, *Eccentricities of a Nightingale*, and *Vieux Carré* the frustrations of the friend who wants to make love, and the difficulties of the beloved who does not, are the occasion of shame, anger, and glorious speech.

> NIGHTINGALE: I've come to expect and almost to accept as if God—the alleged—had stamped on me a sign at birth —"This man will offer himself and not be accepted, not by anyone ever!"
>
> (from *Vieux Carré*)

Friendship in a play by Williams is declared as vehemently as love, and if necessary with force:

GEORGE: Keep your rutten hand off my shoulder.
RALPH: Break it off me. I'm sorry I ridiculed your affliction.
GEORGE: [*Pause: Apology accepted.*]

(from *Period of Adjustment*)

Forceful friendship, like much else in Williams, is based on gentle handling, a little willful deafness or cloudy vision, the haze of a drink or two. The full light of examination can blight friendship, as it does for Brick and the unseen Skipper in *Cat on a Hot Tin Roof.* "The special quality of hell is to see everything clearly down to the last detail," Mishima wrote in his novel *The Temple of the Golden Pavilion*. Dim light allows Blanche in *Streetcar* to seem virginal, permits the aging Nightingale to visit the young Writer in *Vieux Carré,* and allows the Writer to pass for Mrs. Wire's friend as he sits beside her in the dark.

For Williams, on stage and off, friends fantasize their hopes for each other. In their writing and in their lives, his circle of friends charted Heaven and Hell as alternate worlds of delight and terror, just on the other side of the hospital bed in Mishima's *Lady Aoi* or down the stairs to Inge's *The Boy in the Basement*. An excruciating one-act by Williams sums up friendship with its title *I Can't Imagine Tomorrow* and the horror of crawling "in this country of endured but unendurable pain [where] each one is so absorbed, deafened, blinded by his own journey across it, he sees, he looks for, no one else crawling across it with him."

Along with much else, what Tennessee Williams, Carson McCullers, Yukio Mishima, Jane Bowles, and William Inge shared with each other, with readers, and with theater-goers, is a vision that lonely we may be, wounded, hurt, unable to heal each other, yet aware if not always comforted by awareness, that we might soar or float, perhaps with liquor, with words, with sex, or with other illusions, into other worlds of delight and through this one of pain, alone together as friends.

2015

Tenn Years: Tennessee Williams in Provincetown, 2006–2015

Broadway producers and a Hollywood star come to Provincetown to meet a young Tennessee Williams in Something Cloudy, Something Clear, *InterArt Theater Company, (left to right) Brian Runbeck as Mr. Fiddler, Christina Pastor as Mrs. Fiddler, Maria Deasy as Caroline, directed by Cosmin Chivu. Photo by Antonis Achilleos*

In the background, the ruins of the last Provincetown Playhouse.

What happened to Tennessee Williams in Provincetown during the last ten years, 2006 to 2015? Not Thomas Lanier Williams, who passed away in early 1983, but Tennessee Williams, "that nonexistent personage who bears my professional name" as Thomas Lanier Williams (born in 1911) wrote in his *Memoirs*. That nonexistent personage, Tennessee Williams, lives on every time someone attends a performance of what Thomas Lanier Williams wrote.

The answer to the question—What happened to Tennessee Williams in Provincetown during the last ten years?—is that fifty-eight plays he wrote were performed there, ten of them posthumous world premieres, at the annual Provincetown Tennessee Williams Theater Festival.

Since 2006 in Provincetown, on the last weekend of September, plays by Williams have been performed on the beach, in the dunes, inside historic homes, outside historic homes, on porches, inside hotel rooms and hotel lobbies, bars, basements, and dance floors, outside hotels on lawns and around pool decks, in museums, in the Episcopal church, the Unitarian meetinghouse, at Provincetown's Town Hall, at the Cabral family's Fisherman's Wharf, and at Duarte's garage on Bradford Street two years after it was turned into the Provincetown Theater.

Plays by Williams that had been previously ignored or dismissed were performed at the Festival. Estimations of his experiments in form and style based on reading a review, rather than reading or watching a play, were revised by experience. The mantra that Williams lost his mojo in 1964, after *The Milk Train Doesn't Stop Here Anymore* closed on Broadway, fell silent at the world premieres in Provincetown of *Green Eyes* (1970) and *The Remarkable Rooming-House of Mme. Le Monde* (1982).

The tired idea that you had to be from where the action of a play is set to understand it—or perform it—was put to rest as audiences in Provincetown relished interpretations of the *Eccentricities of a Nightingale* from Hong Kong, *The Two-Character Play* from London, *A Streetcar Named Desire* from New Zealand, and a heart-stopping *Milk Train* from Cape Town, South Africa.

The proposition that Williams stopped writing what was called lyric realism because he was alcohol-impaired was overturned by Festival performances of Williams' dialogue in which broken sentences and aching pauses demonstrated virtuosic control and mature musicality. So-called "failures" were reassessed. Late autobiographical plays such as *The Traveling Companion* and *Something Cloudy, Something Clear* were not marginal after all, but essential.

People who saw *Camino Real* or *Orpheus Descending* at the tip of the Cape disagreed with the idea that these plays were inscrutable, as had been declared in the 1950s when both plays opened on Broadway. In Provincetown, audiences wept at *Orpheus*. As John Guare wrote after seeing *Camino Real* performed outdoors in Provincetown with five actors playing eighty-four roles, "The play ended in evening shadows. The bitter cold returned us to an unforgiving reality. And yet we went on. We had been through an experience. We were restored to our old world with new eyes. The Aquarium Wharf became the Globe theater—Tennessee's *teatrum mundi*."

Since well before Williams' death, knowing four plays and a film script by Williams had been considered information enough to dismiss or ignore the rest of his writing. Over time, with even less effort, people could claim expertise by watching four out of those five as films: *A Streetcar Named Desire*, *Cat on a Hot Tin*

Roof, Baby Doll and *Night of the Iguana*. Productions of *The Glass Menagerie* or *Streetcar* on stage from high schools to Broadway passed along clichés of Southern belles shaken by their past, longing for love, distracted by sullen studs. All of this was laughable enough to inspire parodies, and simple enough for biographers to reduce what little they knew about the body of Williams' work to indications of a mental disorder: the love that dare not speak its name.

Concentrating on the playwright's life, drinking habits, or sexuality, avoided engagement—exhilarating, challenging, and life-affirming rather than library-affirming engagement—with what Williams actually wrote. It was easier to declare Tennessee Williams symptomatically Southern, or gay, or to define him by the French Quarter of New Orleans, or the Mississippi Delta, or a three month stay at the Barnes Clinic in St. Louis.

Williams' identity, however, as performances in Provincetown made clear, is not anything so limited. If we had to slap on a label, it would be American, in the tradition of Walt Whitman, whose poem "Pioneers! O Pioneers!" defines what it means to be American as the camaraderie of lovers and the outcast:

All the hands of comrades clasping, all the Southern, all the Northern…

Most of the plays by Williams staged in Provincetown were set outside Dixie: in Manhattan and the Midwest, occasionally in New Mexico, Japan, Italy, England, and New England. Williams wrote over a hundred plays between 1930 (*Beauty is the Word*) and 1983 (*The One Exception*) and most of those were set outside Dixie, too.

He experimented constantly. Within the context of five decades of writing, Williams' sixteen years of commercial success were an aberration. Few of the plays Williams wrote were originally intended to be staged with the realism of 1940s and '50s moviemaking.

Directors coming to Provincetown restored what Williams intended: the phantasmagoria to *Streetcar*, the Kabuki stage hands to *Milk Train*, and the shape-shifting to *Camino Real*. The bitter humor and sexual freedom of the plays Williams wrote in the 1970s and early '80s, after he turned sixty, played in Provincetown with gusto, upending, among other pieties, motherly love, as in this stage direction from *Mme. Le Monde*:

> [Mme. Le Monde abruptly floors her son with a lethal karate chop. This action is startling even to Hall. He lifts the youth's wrist which is pulseless.]
> Hall: Was this your only offspring, Mme. Le Monde?
> Mme. Le Monde: Mr. Hall, my fecundity is equal to the queen bee's. I am constantly reproducing drones such as that one.

For too long, scholars fascinated by manuscript variations lost their curiosity for understanding plays in performance, as if one could offer a respectable opinion about bicycles, never having ridden one, by taking a magnifying glass to a photograph of Lance Armstrong. The Festival in Provincetown attracted scholars who studied and wrote about performance. Critical reassessments of plays previously unknown in performance have appeared in articles and books over the last ten years. Interpretations and approaches to Williams' work have expanded, and Williams' reputation has changed since 2006, in part due to the conversations between artists and scholars, before, during, and after Provincetown productions.

Is there anything about Provincetown itself that encouraged any of this to happen? Yes, the same things that helped and encouraged Thomas Lanier Williams when he was living there for four summers in the 1940s.

To begin with, Provincetown's leading industry, tourism, makes the lion's share of its profits in a season that begins the Fourth of July weekend and ends on Labor Day. There is an art to living well year-round on Cape Cod by stretching the season's haul over twelve months, not unlike the process by which, in Williams' blazing *Suddenly Last Summer,* a poet's mother announces that her son Sebastian writes poetry. As she reads the title of Sebastian's last book she explains that his life was his work and his work was his life:

> Mrs. Venable: *Poem of Summer,* and the date of the summer, there are twenty-five of them, he wrote one poem a year.... One for each summer that we traveled together. The other nine months of the year were really only a preparation.

Any play or a poem by Williams functions this way, the way fine wine, honey, or a fire from a burning log releases the stored-up energy of the sun. In a play by Williams, love and beauty and youth don't last; there's an imperative to recall them. They're like the heat of summer remembered "in the winter of cities," as Williams first book of poetry was titled. Think of the plays by Williams that take place in the summer, as the Kabuki stagehands say in *Milk Train*:

> under that, that—angry old lion, the sun.

And usually—as the subtitle title for *The Parade* has it—*Approaching the End of a Summer*:

> As the summer approaches the end of the summer—have you noticed? —The sunsets from the dunes become more spectacular than ever. —Endings, approaches to endings…

It's fitting that the Festival is in September, when it's time in Provincetown to reflect on a season's gains and losses. It's the time when Williams himself moved on. Twice he missed a September hurricane, and in the years since 2006 performances of his plays have—so far—dodged any major storms like the one that sent the ruins of the last Provincetown Playhouse collapsing into the bay a few weeks after Williams left town in 1944.

The liminality of the land at the tip of the Cape is literal: the sand crumbles into the sea. At evening the horizon blurs, the colors of the sky and sea merge, the eye crosses easily over sea to sky and back again. The plays of the 2015 season have in common a similar crossing over (and back) between the physical world to the world of the spirit. This is expressed by slipping off costumes and wigs (as in *Milk Train*), walking through curtains of paper (as in *The Day on Which a Man Dies*), and by taking a ride off the highway (in *The Case of the Crushed Petunias*). All of these are voyages to another way of seeing, being, loving, thinking. Or dissolving, as it's described in *Talk To Me Like the Rain and Let Me Listen*, spoken as a guitar plays:

> Woman: I'll go out and walk on the esplanade. I'll walk alone and be blown thinner and thinner…And thinner and thinner and thinner and thinner and thinner! —Till finally I won't have any body at all, and the wind picks me up in its cool white arms forever, and takes me away!

That it is possible—without being picked up by the wind—to travel to another world is suggested by the mix of people one meets walking up and down the narrow Provincetown streets. When Williams was here, fishermen and artists, freckled Yankees and tanned Azoreans, sailors and drag queens—even in the 1940s—shared the town. Their paths were not so separate as in Mississippi, where Williams was born, with its state enforced segregation of black and white. In Provincetown, as in New Orleans, the city of *laissez les bons temps rouler*, there's mingling. Within sight of the bay through which the Pilgrims walked ashore from the Mayflower, in Provincetown, as in Mississippi or in New Orleans, the intensity of the present moment is enhanced by one's sense of the past.

In 1944 Williams settled into a shack on the Provincetown beach to finish his play *The Gentlemen Caller*, which would soon be titled *The Glass Menagerie*. What money he had ran out—money he had saved from his job as a screenwriter at MGM. In photographs from the summer of 1944, Williams is noticeably thinner. The fishermen, who did notice, provided him with fish and potatoes. That generosity persists. For one week a year, for ten years, the inn owners of Provincetown have donated rooms, in some years a hundred rooms, for Festival artists and staff. Other businesses donate food for actors and bicycles for crew members to get around town. Most venues for Festival events are donated.

That continuity of spirit and space underwrites the Provincetown Tennessee Williams Theater Festival, as does the physical beauty of the place, and the sensibility of its artist's colony.

Attracted by the sunlight bouncing over sand and water, in 1899 the painter Charles Hawthorne (who wintered in Paris and New York), started the Cape Cod School of Art in Provincetown, passing on the impressionist practice of painting outdoors. By 1916, when the twenty-seven-year-old fledgling playwright Eugene O'Neill arrived, he might have read in the *Boston Globe* that there were six art schools, and three hundred artists were living in town, twenty-five of them year-round.

An artist's colony had grown up, attracting writers, actors, musicians, and political radicals. O'Neill wrote for the art colony's theater, the original Provincetown Playhouse, where the scenery was designed and built by fine artists, among them the painters Charles Demuth (who also acted) and Marsden Hartley. For O'Neill's *Bound East for Cardiff*, the sculptor/painter William Zorach suggested Cubist scenery; O'Neill insisted on kitchen-sink realism and the play was performed with the bay door of the former wharf-house pulled back so that the fog specified by O'Neill's stage directions could roll in.

Then as now, discussions of art influenced ideas of theater. In Provincetown, when O'Neill was there, experiments in theatrical form and style were thought of in the context of Cubism and Expressionism, a hundred years later in the context of Jackson Pollock and Hans Hofmann's color theory.

In the 1930s the sophistication of the town was enhanced by the arrival of German refugees, Hofmann and the performance artist Valeska Gert among them. The art colony's sense of a connection to the wider world, spurred by intense study of what's in front of your nose, resonates in *Aimez-Vous Ionesco?*, the 2015 world premiere one-act by Williams, in which two matrons ogle a handsome young dancer:

> Francine: You're not even looking at him. What are you looking at?
> Delphine: The stage of the City Center, my own, built in me.
> Francine: I'm looking at Isadora Duncan dancing on the Acropolis, in the Parthenon, and at Vaslav Nijinsky practicing on the boat that took him to South America…

It has been understood for over a hundred years in Provincetown that pushing boundaries in writing and painting means pushing boundaries of identity and social liberties. Performed in Provincetown, Williams' celebrations of sexuality are political, metaphoric, and enjoyed. Being queer, in any sense of the word, has a history in Provincetown that dates back to right after the Pilgrims abandoned the place and those who would escape Puritanism crept back. The tip of the Cape was too far away from Boston for the sheriff to come regularly. It's still too far away for the sheriffs of good taste.

Then and now, people come to the tip of Cape Cod to escape, to be forgotten, to center themselves in the sight of the sea and the sky, to open their minds, to lose their hearts, to lick their wounds, to make love, to be left alone to write or paint or brood. By November the ferry doesn't run, the waves are too choppy; the pilots of the Cape Air nine-seaters decline on occasion to confront the wind. In all seasons the highway is one lane each way between Dennis and Orleans, and when it snows the driving is dangerous and slow.

The isolation of the town accelerated soon after Williams arrived in 1940, when the train tracks were ripped up beyond Hyannis and the land where the train ran was sold. In the ten years between 2006 and 2015 the place has become increasingly isolated. The high school has closed for lack of students. In the winter of 2015 the population was probably less than 900. More than half the 2,500 people who claim legal residence in Provincetown spend the coldest months in warmer places.

Loss echoes in Provincetown along the deserted winter streets and beaches. Loss shadows the summer here, too, and has for decades. The end of the fishing industry in the 1930s was as devastating as a great hurricane would have been. The advent of AIDS in the 1980s hit Provincetown just as hard, and for anyone who came here at that time and after there are reminders of who and what is gone.

Great loss in a play by Williams—Belle Reve, the plantation Stella and Blanche talk about in *Streetcar*—reminds us of our own lost beautiful dreams. Many roles in the plays of the 2015 season are defined by loss: Mrs. Venable and her son in *Suddenly Last Summer*, the diva and her beauty in *Milk Train*, the lover and his beloved in *The Parade*, the artist and his talent in *Day on Which a Man Dies*:

> Man: Where are they, where did they go, the images, the visions?
> [*A Stage Assistant opens the panel again to reveal an abstract design of birds in flight.*]
> Man: —*They say if* you wait for them, they'll come back.

Most of the 2015 adaptations from William' writings have "happy endings." In Spatfeather Theatre's *The Liberation of Colette Simple*, based on Williams' short play *The Case of the Crushed Petunias*, a caged canary flies free. In John Guare's *More Stars*

Than There Are In Heaven, based on the Williams short story "The Mattress by the Tomato Patch," the young writer's future success is revealed. Carson Efird's dance steps, inspired by Williams' diaries, trace a *Road to Paradise*, but end with a hell of a letter sent from 534 Commercial Street on July 12, 1941, in which Williams wrote, "What a mad house I am in! I may return to New York before this letter reaches you, as the situation here is intolerable."

In contrast, when a play by Williams ends we comprehend what Williams called the catastrophe of success. The long awaited Gentleman Caller (luck, happiness, fulfillment) arrives, but he is engaged to someone else, as in *The Glass Menagerie*. Or, as in *Aimez-Vous Ionesco?*, when Mr. Coppitt walks in, he asks to use the chamber pot, does so and leaves, but not before looking at himself in the mirror—and he is worth admiring.

When what's admirable is gone, it's worth recalling, like a splendid summer day recalled in September, or Williams' visions recalled by performances in Provincetown for the last ten Septembers. Loss sometimes prompts an imperative to recall.

TENN YEARS

Occasional Essays

Hotel Plays Photographic Essay

In Mach 2015, Ride Hamilton photographed *The Hotel Plays*, a collection of short plays by Tennessee Williams, performed in the rooms, hallways, staircases, staircase landings, and gardens of the Hermann-Grima House in the French Quarter of New Orleans as part of the New Orleans/Tennessee Williams Literary Festival.

In certain of Hamilton's photographs, faces are unclear or in shadow, parts of the image are out of focus. The color has been stripped to sepia, or filtered to yellow with whiffs of deep brown and delicate blue. Some images are dark, an invitation to the luxury of looking closely and for a long time. As often as not the performers are not performing, but thinking, waiting, watching. Mirrors, doors, windows—either opened or closed—staircases, shadows, glare, all of these access a world of the spirit.

The house was built in 1831 for use by a single family. Over time it became a boardinghouse. Now it is a museum. Staging plays there is like playing music on a keyboard that has keys to play notes that can't be heard, but can be felt.

Robert Mitchell, waiting between performances of Mister Paradise, *in the upper staircase landing of the Hermann-Grima House Museum, New Orleans 2015. From* The Hotel Plays, *directed by David Kaplan. Photo by Ride Hamilton.*

The Last of My Solid Gold Watches *in the Hermann-Grima House Museum, Joel Derby as Bob Harper. New Orleans 2015. From* The Hotel Plays, *directed by David Kaplan. Photo by Ride Hamilton.*

Desiree Ledet waiting to perform Mrs. Wire in The Lady of Larkspur Lotion *in the lower hall of the Hermann-Grima House Museum, New Orleans 2015. From* The Hotel Plays, *directed by David Kaplan. Photo by Ride Hamilton.*

Francesca McKenzie waiting to enter as The Girl in Mister Paradise, *in the lower hall of the Hermann-Grima House Museum, New Orleans 2015. From* The Hotel Plays, *directed by David Kaplan. Photo by Ride Hamilton.*

The Last of My Solid Gold Watches, *the Hermann-Grima House Museum, New Orleans 2015. Joel Derby as Bob Harper, George Sanchez as Mr. Charlie Colton. From* The Hotel Plays, *directed by David Kaplan. Photo by Ride Hamilton.*

The Hotel Plays

For five decades, from the mid-1930s to the early 1980s, Tennessee Williams wrote short plays set in hotel rooms or boardinghouses. A dozen of these plays run about twenty minutes each. They often take place in New Orleans, sometimes in St. Louis, or the Mississippi Delta, sometimes in Manhattan. There's usually a bed in the room and someone is usually in it or on it. Since 2009 in Provincetown we have called them "the hotel plays."

It's irresistible to connect the settings of the plays to the playwright's life in hotels. Rich and famous or poor and unknown, clothed or not, on a bender or typing for hours, Williams spent much of his life in hotels. He died in a hotel room, as did Eugene O'Neill, who was born in one, too. Williams first stayed in New Orleans in an attic in what was called a "crib" separated from another crib with a dirty hanging sheet. He eventually owned a comfortable suite in the upscale *Elysée* Hotel on the Upper East Side where he took his own life. Despite the difference in décor,

The Last of My Solid Gold Watches, in the Hermann-Grima House Museum, New Orleans 2015. Drew Calhoun as The Porter, George Sanchez as Mr. Charlie Colton. From The Hotel Plays, *directed by David Kaplan. Detail of a photo by Ride Hamilton.*

both offered him what the proprietor of the "Ritz Men Only" on the Camino Real offers:

A little white ship to sail the dangerous night in…

Williams' 1930s boardinghouse life in New Orleans under the eye of an overbearing landlady, echoed his home life in St. Louis with his overbearing mother. Did he unconsciously fall into the familiar pattern because it gave him an identity as wayward son? Did living in poverty gain him compassion for the outcasts of society, something his middle-class life in the Midwest had not? Did the anonymity of hotels, rich and poor, allow him sexual freedom? Are hotels then, for Williams, the sites where the possibilities of art and life intersected?

Yes, yes, yes, and maybe. As always, after vivisecting Williams' writing in the laboratories of biography, psychology, sociology, or identity politics, the plays are left gasping for air. Williams, for all his reconstruction of himself and his circumstances into drama (on stage and off), is a mythic writer, mythic in the sense that he offers a vision of the physical world and its circumstances shadowed by a parallel world of the spirit and fate. An awareness of Williams' myth expands the significance of the hotel plays beyond symptoms of class or sexuality to a meaning made even clearer by the title Williams proposed for his autobiography: *Flee, Flee this Sad Hotel*. Put inelegantly, for Williams a hotel room is the body, the temporary residence of the soul. The soul has come from somewhere unknown (in a Hotel Play, off stage), and goes to somewhere unknown (in a Hotel Play, off stage). What we see in eighteen minutes, sometimes fifteen, less than twenty, are souls on a time-out, given or grabbing a respite, hiding from death, heroically defying death by speaking out or by remaining silent, or for meeting an appointment with death. To be in the hotel room is to be in a state of suspension, like a trance. Outside, waiting, is the enemy: time.

The sound of the enemy is a Hotel Play's score: the tick of fifteen solid-gold watches, the knocks at the door, the thump of a faulty heart, the clump of a cane striking the ground, the patter of rain. The hypnotic repetition is disrupted by the call of the outside world—a chauffeur's horn, a jangling doorbell—reminding whomever is inside that it's time to go forth. The sound of death waiting outside can be as overt as ambulance sirens that echo on Central Park West in *The Traveling Companion* and the creak of a trapdoor which opens up to hell (via the London sewers) in the *Remarkable Rooming-House of Mme. Le Monde*.

In the early hotel plays, groaning doors keep out or open onto a hostile world we hear about but do not need to see because it is our world, where we sit in the audience: war-ridden, angry, and passive. Inside the hotel room there's defiance of death and time—and if that defiance is a lie, the time the lie takes to be told staves off death for that much longer. The words cast that much of a spell.

As so often in plays written by Tennessee Williams, what we see repudiates what we hear. Tales of a fancy party are windy boasts in a seedy hot room with a broken fan; the hopeful diary of a young girl in Greece is read aloud by a feral spinster in the French Quarter, the young girl described in the diary as fresh and flirty is, in the play, a crone hiding behind a curtain; a gold-edged little book of inspiring verse is held uncomfortably close to the wreck of the poet who wrote it; a titled lady and the bed of a failed playwright both have lice, which may or may not have been intended as a pun for lies. In *The Last of My Solid Gold Watches*, hope is literally fading in a framed lithograph titled "Blind-folded Hope clutches a broken lyre." Is lyre intended as another pun?

The shrouded women, the rotting cloth, the maiden with the lyre, the ticking clock, the doors that close or open on a tomb are the hallmarks of another definitive American poet. What seems like hyperbole in *A Streetcar Named Desire*, when Blanche looks at Stella's apartment, is a deflected observation of the city of New Orleans.

Only Poe! Only Mr. Edgar Allan Poe!—could do it justice!

Blanche, with a gesture to the window goes on:

Out there I suppose is the ghoul-haunted woodland of Weir!

Williams knew ghoul-haunted New Orleans inside and out, by sight and by smell: the rotting old wood and velvet, the rusting old iron, the blackened silver, the decaying old families in bejeweled gaslit ruins , the former beauties—male and female— the has-been poets, the poets that never were. Poe's poetic fiction was Williams' poetic reality.

At the same time, and in the same city, the photographer, Clarence John Laughlin (who is sometimes called the Edgar Allan Poe of photographers) documented the same ghastliness: stuffed birds, funereal curtains, ironically crumbling columns, old ladies, older ladies, bewildered children. The art of Laughlin's photographs captures, simultaneously, the picturesque present, the spirit of the past, and the form of the eternal. The same could be said for the wooden boxes made by Joseph Cornell in Astoria, Queens, that they trap the ephemeral and the eternal together. Cornell and Tennessee Williams met in the early 1930s through a mutual friend, the author Donald Windham. Cornell's "A White Crested Cockatoo (for Blanche DuBois)," created in 1948, is dedicated to Tennessee Williams.

Considering Cornell's work reveals the way Williams works. Within his boxes Cornell assembled bits of paper, glass, metal springs, marbles, and other detritus. The shattered remnants resting in their container evoke a glorious whole, irretrievably gone. In a similar way inside hotel rooms Williams arranges bits of lives, their former glories gone, though glory might glimmer or blaze up. In a process known as distressing, Cornell buried his boxes in the earth and then dug them up, another reminder of Poe.

Cornell made over thirty boxes with Hotel themes. They resemble stage sets waiting for someone to enter, or stage sets after all the actors have left. Sometimes Cornell's hotel is a birdcage with a perch and a parrot. In Cornell's "Toward the Blue Peninsula (for Emily Dickinson)," the perch is empty, a window in the cage is open, the bird has flown out. The subject of the sculpture is what's not there, but we know has been there before, in other words, a ghost image.

Laughlin was more direct in conjuring ghosts for his photographs. He would stage scenes with models and props posed in ruins. The titles of Laughlin's *tableaux vivants* could be summaries of Williams' hotel plays: "The Image of the Past," "The Repulsive Bed," "The Closet of the Past," "Elegy for the Old South." Williams and Laughlin knew some of the same people in New Orleans. Eloi Bordeleon, the model for the role of Eloi (pronounced EL-wah) in Williams' *Auto-da-Fé*, was photographed by Laughlin, including a few shiny 8 x 10s where Eloi in a dapper suit points to a slightly warped unframed painting of Saint Joseph with the baby Jesus. We can imagine him delivering some of Williams' lines from *Auto-da-Fé* :

ELOI: This fetid old swamp we live in, the Vieux Carré! Every imaginable kind of degeneracy springs up here, not at arm's length, even, but right in our presence!

Eloi's disgust with the Quarter is part of a pattern. To counter spellbinding storytelling in a hotel room, Williams placed an unbeliever, someone disinterested, or skeptical or sleepy or, more melodramatically, someone provoked by lies and eager to expose them. In *Larkspur Lotion*, the landlady isn't buying the reasons why her rent hasn't been paid; in *Solid Gold Watches* the young salesman reads comic books rather than paying attention to an old man's advice. In *Lord Byron's Love Letter* the tipsy tourist is more interested in the passing parade than dead poets, and in a reversal the title character of *Mister Paradise*, the creator/poet, like Prospero, disavows his own powers. In *The Traveling Companion* and *Sunburst*, the eloquence of elders is lost on feral young men intent on making money by hustling or robbery. What is striking is the continuity of design from the earliest hotel plays to the hotel plays Williams was working on in the months before he died. Invariably, the magic wins—the spell takes effect, the landlady retreats, the poet grants an audience and imparts at least one more poem. The feral youngsters are beguiled, if ironically, in *Sunburst*, written in the early 1980s and published posthumously. Williams has the wit to let an old Broadway diva recite enough Shakespeare to bore her would-be thieves to sleep, allowing her to be rescued.

Whoever speaks in a Hotel Play wields power over who listens: the kidnappers slumber in *Sunburst*; in *The Pink Bedroom* an unwanted lover departs; the spiritualist's sermons raise money in *Thank You, Kind Spirit*; the young wife's filthy talk in *Green Eyes* conjures her husband's sex drive; the Writer's confession in *Larkspur Lotion* shames his landlady enough that she exits without extracting any rent.

The earliest hotel plays set out Tennessee Williams' compassionate preoccupations in speeches as florid as Shakespeare's early history plays where, as in Williams early plays, proclamation can overwhelm character.

> The motion of life is upwards, the motion of death is down. Only the blindest of all blind fools can fail to see which is going to be finally—highest up! Not death, but life, my dear. Life—*life*! I defy them to stop it forever! Not with all their guns, not with all their destruction! We will keep on singing. Someday the air all over the earth will be full of our singing. [*A horn sounds.*]
>
> (from *Mister Paradise*)

Dialogue spoken in the later hotel plays is often as spare and disjointed as in a play by Samuel Beckett. The defiance of death is frequent, and witty, and in performance, the exposed bodies of the older performers—Williams often has them in their underwear—

moves us to think of endurance, the actors', the character's, and the playwright's.

> Being unable to go on alone and having no way to go back to—where would I go back to?
>
> (from The Traveling Companion)

As in a play by Beckett or Chekhov, one can't go on—one goes on. Hotel rooms are for transients, pun intended. In the audience of a Hotel Play, we share with the actors a mutual resistance to the enemy time, scored by the sound of our own beating hearts.

NOTES

A partial list of hotel plays: *The Lady of Larkspur Lotion*, *Thank You Kind Spirit*, *Mister Paradise*, and *Green Eyes* are all set in the French Quarter, the first three written between 1940 and '41, the last one in 1970; *The Pink Bedroom* and *Hello from Bertha* were both written in the early 1940s and set in East St. Louis. The New York hotel plays include *Talk to Me Like the Rain and Let Me Listen*, written in the 1950s and set in Hell's Kitchen, and *The Traveling Companion*, written in the later 1970s and set at the upscale Essex House and the posthumously published *Sunburst*, written in the early 1980s. *The Last of My Solid Gold Watches*, written in the early 1940s, is set in the Mississippi, where Williams was born. The still unpublished—a page is missing—*Once in a Lifetime*, also written around 1940, is set in the lobby of an Albuquerque motor lodge. There are more hotel plays written by Williams in archives.

There are some longer one-act plays written by Williams set in hotel rooms and boardinghouses: *The Mutilated*, situated precisely on New Orleans' seedy South Rampart Street; *The Remarkable Rooming-House of Mme Le Monde* takes place high in a London garret; *The Strangest Kind of Romance* is in a Midwestern boarding-house with a view of a smoke-spewing factory. *The Day on Which a Man Dies* is mostly set in adjoining rooms of a Tokyo hotel. There are seven full-length plays by Williams with hotel settings: the sound of scratching in *The Night of the Iguana* comes from under the deck of "a rather rustic and very Bohemian hotel, the Costa Verde" on the West coast of Mexico. *Sweet Bird of Youth* pulls back the covers at "the elegant old Royal Palms Hotel in the town of St. Cloud" on the Gulf Coast; *Summer and Smoke* and *The Eccentricities of a Nightingale* climax in the rooms for rent above Mississippi's notorious Moon Lake Casino. *Camino Real* boasts the deluxe Siete Mares—Spanish for the *Seven Seas*—opposite the low-rent "Ritz Men Only" at the dead end of a highway in Latin America; *Clothes for a Summer Hotel* takes its title from scenes in the Reve Bleu, the blue dream of a 1920s hideaway on the Côte d'Azur. *Vieux Carré* is set at 722 Toulouse Street in the old French Quarter, the address of the first New Orleans boardinghouse where Williams roomed in 1939.

In Joseph Cornell's diaries between 1951 to 1970 Cornell refers to "Hotel Pelican," "Hotel de l'Univers," "Hotel Observatoire," "Hotel Savoi," "Hotel de l'Univers #2," "Hotel s. Lumiere (Gozzoli de Medici)," Hotel de L'Etoile,' Hotel Du Bon Port," "Hotel Andromeda," "Hotel Valencia," "Voyageur's Hotel," "Hotel Tudor," "Hotel des Etrangers," "Star Hotel," and the "Hotel of the Golden Bee."

The Last of My Solid Gold Watches, *in the Hermann-Grima House Museum, New Orleans 2015. Drew Calhoun as The Porter, George Sanchez as Mr. Charlie Colton. From* The Hotel Plays, *directed by David Kaplan. Detail of a photo by Ride Hamilton.*

One Arm in South Africa: "Stirring Up Feelings Without Feeling Nothing" Myself

You want to know what's going on in *One Arm*? It's Tennessee Williams imagining what his whores think. What's gliding underneath that smooth skin other than shadowy blue muscles? Does the animal he desires have a soul like his? Or is that animal something different? Something inhuman? Something we don't recognize as human?

Consider male beauties of very few words in those famous Williams plays: Brick in *Cat on a Hot Tin Roof*, or Doctor Sugar in *Suddenly Last Summer*, or John Buchanan in *Summer and Smoke* and *Eccentricities of a Nightingale*. These are problematic roles, as anyone knows who has tried to act them (or direct the plays in which they appear), because these guys, "as sparkling cold

"Degra-desperation" is the word coined by a girl to describe her life shacking up with a smooth-skinned petty thief who works nights as a barker for a Bourbon Street strip-show. I Never Get Dressed Till After Dark on Sundays, *The Infinite Theatre, Jack Kesy as Tye, directed by Nick Potenzieri. TW Fest 2012. Photo by Josh Andrus.*

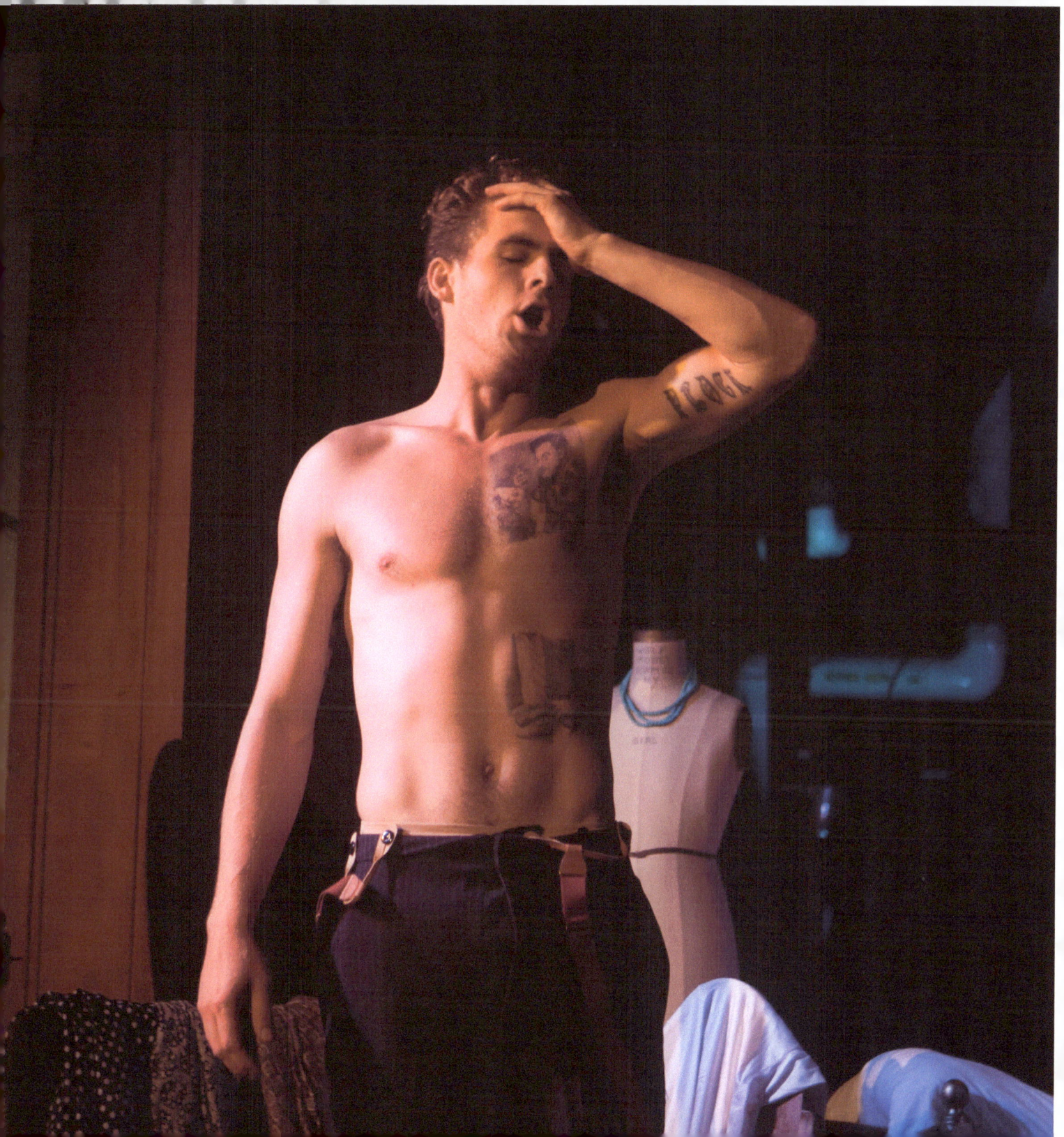

as branches after an ice storm," as Miss Alma describes John Buchanan, seem becalmed. Yet everyone chattering nervously on stage in their presence is waiting to see and hear what these withholding studs will say or do. By staying mum, men control the situation and bring out the spoken truth or the desperation of a bitch-in-heat from whoever's had the misfortune to want something from them. Just so Ollie Winemiller in *One Arm*.

Ollie is well endowed by his creator. Williams gave Ollie the callipygian ass of Kip Kiernan (the first and maybe only man Williams fell in love with without reserve), which is helpfully defined in the text, "narrow hips with high, prominent buttocks." He has Kip's marble-white skin. He has the champion lightweight boxer's body of Kilroy from Williams' *Camino Real*. "Not a bad-looking boy," says the Gypsy in that play. "It's no use saying to you good luck," says the Gypsy in *One Arm*.

In the Abrahamse/Meyer adaptation of *One Arm* for the stage in South Africa, Ollie has also been gifted with Williams' narrative voice and a poem Williams wrote about the electric chair. Articulate whores—in history and fiction—are more usually female. Having Ollie use words like *dilemma* grants him a vocabulary Tennessee Williams reserved for himself, but also hooks Ollie up with Chance Wayne and Valentine Xavier, the pretty-faced sweet-talking hustlers in Williams' *Sweet Bird of Youth* and *Orpheus Descending*.

"He's mighty good looking," drawls the man that Val's cuckolding, before sizing up Val (short for Valentine) as trouble.

Discovering what's beneath your own skin is the real discovery of *One Arm*, for Williams and Ollie. As Williams has Ollie say, he was "stirring up feelings without feeling nothing myself." When a murder Ollie committed makes headlines, former clients—furtive men with fictitious names—seeing his unforgettable face in the newspapers, write letters to him on death row, letters confessing that his brief hours with them were the richest in their lives. Ollie reads those letters over and over and, when he enters the death chamber to be electrocuted, he carries the letters with him as a child would a doll and keeps them so firmly clamped between his legs when he sits down on the hot seat that the guards choose not to pull them out. Think about that as an image to combine what's between a hustler's legs and what's between his ears. Like a good actor, Ollie gains character by how he understands someone other than himself. The pages probably catch on fire when the current passes through him.

That life or love is a flash in the dark is Tennessee Williams' ultimate metaphor: a girl blowing out a candle or a man lighting a cigarette. What shines so briefly demands to be remembered: faces and glittering eyes picked out in the gloom, as in film noir cinematography, or a painting by Caravaggio, the painter who invited the puffy-lipped Roman hustlers of the 1600s to sit for him as his models for pagan gods (Narcissus! Bacchus!) and various Catholic Saints. In the seventeenth century, the 1940s, and now, those who make paintings, film, short stories, and plays, and those who inspire them, are illuminations of the Buddhist idea that the lotus blooms best in the mud.

That juxtaposed binaries make for dynamic opposition (Valentine Xavier, for example, Eros/Christ) is something Williams learned a lot about from Erwin Piscator at the New School's Theater Department in Manhattan and from Hans Hofmann at Hofmann's art school in Provincetown. In interviews Williams sometimes defined his own life as an ongoing bout between a Puritan killjoy and a Cavalier who lived for pleasure. In the climactic scene of the short story, "One Arm," (and the frame of the Abrahamse/Meyer stage adaptation) a Lutheran minister, sitting opposite Ollie, tells a dream about a hungry panther. Seeing both together, like hearing Ollie speak with Williams' voice, acquaints the Puritan with the Cavalier, not to commingle but to contend. Even though Ollie explains that the door down the hallway creaks and no one could catch them at whatever it is they might be up to, when Ollie offers the crack of his callipygian ass for a rubdown, the terrified minister calls a prison guard. It's easier for the minister to join Ollie in a death chant than in pleasure. They share the verses of a poem about the electric chair instead. And that, after all, is the light source, the illumination, the action, of Williams' grace: pain or pleasure, to share.

Mink Stole as Trinket besotted with Jack Noble as Slim in The Mutilated, *Beth Bartley Productions/Inter-Art Group, New York City. Directed by Cosmin Chivu. TW Fest 2013. Photo by Josh Andrus.*

The Day On Which A Man Dies: Reading the Red in Tennessee Williams

Words are
A net to catch
Beauty

Tennessee Williams wrote this sideways, perpendicular to the blue lines of his teen-age poet's journal. That longing to capture beauty extended into his mature stagecraft.

The composed musicality of his realistic-seeming dialogue, the aria-like monologues, the memorably beautiful phrases, even in his stage directions, are distinctive aspects of Williams virtuosity.

Williams' use of color in his plays has a special beauty. Most obviously there are the colors described by characters in the play, often in moments of extremis: the Della Robbia blue Blanche

The Day on Which a Man Dies, National Pastime Theatre, Chicago. Jeff Christian as The Man, directed by David Kaplan. TW Fest 2009. Montage photograph by Michael McGowan.

insists is the right name for the color of the jacket she puts on for her final exit in *A Streetcar Named Desire*, the seared white of Catharine's vision in *Suddenly Last Summer*; a man's silk shirt *colore di rose!* in *The Rose Tattoo*.

Williams' control of color seen on stage is also masterful. In *The Day on Which a Man Dies*, begun in 1957 and completed in 1960, the progression of color specified by Williams organizes the meanings of every other aspect of the text: story, characters, behavior, and the anticlimactic structure of the play.

Williams asks that the performance begin with the title of the play projected in Japanese in crimson ideographs. Next, according to the stage directions, the title should appear in English, projected in a vividly contrasting color. The counter-point of red and a contrasting color is the recurring motif of the next seventy-five minutes.

The action starts inside two identical hotel rooms, viewed side by side, like lobes of a brain. Stage right is spare, subdued in color. The other room, stage left, has been converted into a painter's studio. Williams describes it:

> …a room whose effect of violence and disorder, fearfully subjective, is expressed by great stretched canvasses stacked about the walls, all painted in primary colors in abstractions that seem to utter panicky cries.

> The man, the artist, stands over a canvas stretched at his feet. He is holding a spray-gun with which the paint is applied to the canvas. He is breathing as heavily as if he had been in fierce physical combat with the demon inhabiting the canvas beneath.

Images of arteries, muscles, and bone have been painted on the artist's body.

> After a few moments of staring down at the canvas, he sprays it with more red paint, then hurls the spray-gun away and falls to his knees, smearing the paint about the canvas with his fingers: the image fails him. He falls back on his haunches with a sick gasp in his throat.

The wet red paint smeared across the painted organs and bones necessarily evokes catastrophic injury.

Within the first minutes of performance, then, Williams presents the inspiration for this text: the art and death of the painter Jackson Pollock. The painter of *The Day on Which a Man Dies* is no direct portrait—but details are derived from the playwright's direct experience, gossip, and intuition about Pollock, whom Williams had known from the time they summered together in Provincetown in the 1940s. Pollock was killed in 1956 when he drove his car into a tree in East Hampton. Williams, who had done the same thing in Italy with the intent to kill himself, considered Pollock's death a suicide.

Artists and poets who defied convention in order to articulate ecstasy beyond convention, who had intoxicated visions, and who were doomed in their search yet kept searching, were central to Williams' romantic ideas of creation. In some way Williams was haunted by Pollock and other "inspirational" suicides—the American poets Hart Crane and Vachel Lindsay, and Williams' friend, the Japanese writer Yukio Mishima, to whom *The Day on Which a Man Dies* is dedicated.

In *Day on Which,* red is associated with the Promethean impulses of the romantic artist; cool colors and cooler emotions provide a contrasting point of view in the conclusion of the performance. The red advances as the play progresses. The painter, in the process of creation, increasingly covers his body with paint, so that, to the eye, artwork and artist's body become one. Arguing with his mistress, drunk and enraged, he smashes a whiskey bottle, walks barefoot on the glass shards, and tracks bloody footprints across the floor. Bent beneath the force of his mistress's vicious insults, sobbing with his head in his painted hands, the artist's tear-stained face drips with red.

A truce, of sorts, is called, and Williams directs the painter, before visiting his mistress in the next room, to put on a black kimono and slippers. The practical effect is that the red of the painter's body exits—though not completely. The streaks and stains on the painter's face peek above the kimono's neckline. As the couple sits beside each other in silence, a branch of pale flowers is placed onto the stage between them (by a stagehand) as a symbol of reconciliation.

The "round red disk of the risen sun" begins the next scene. The woman rises from bed, revealing that she, also, is painted. If a realistic excuse must be given, the paint from the artist's body would have rubbed off on her during the night's lovemaking.

The two get dressed. The dialogue establishes they are to have lunch in a fashionable part of town. There is no time for either to shower, and so it may be concluded they put their good clothes on over the dried red paint—as if they were camouflaging the night's bruises. In the original production in Chicago, the actor playing the painter washed his face and hands, so that in his suit he appeared without blemish—but the audience understood that beneath the suit his body was an open wound. Stage left, in plain sight of the neutral-colored room with its well-dressed sophisticates, the red-splattered studio lies waiting as an arena for further violence.

After the artist's mistress leaves for lunch, the painter discovers that she has betrayed him. Crushed in spirit, he crosses back into his studio. His natty suit seen against the red splatters silently establishes his alienation from the source of his creativity. Then he speaks:

> MAN: Luck fails and the light goes out: no candles, no matches. —What then? The steady going along with each morning and a day and night? — No…

bear a direct relationship to *Macbeth*'s act 5, scene 5:

> Tomorrow, and tomorrow, and tomorrow,
> Creeps in this petty pace from day to day
> To the last syllable of recorded time,
> And all our yesterdays have lighted fools
> The way to dusty death. Out, out, brief candle!

The painter then kills himself. Williams specifies that at the moment of his death the artist's teeth have drawn blood: another outpouring of red.

The scene shifts abruptly, as does the color. We are on the Ginza, the pretty confetti-colored shopping district of Tokyo. The mistress is having tea. She reflects on the shop signs:

> WOMAN: —These ideographs!…If they put me into an ideograph, I'd be a thing hanging naked, yes, a line-drawing

in colored ink of a naked thing, outlines in cool color but hot color here—and here…[Her gloved hands touch her breasts and groin.]

With this speech, the key to the color in the play has been articulated. It's Hans Hofmann's theories of hot and cold color, which Williams discusses in the novel *Moise and the World of Reason* (1975). At his school in Provincetown, Hofmann taught that paintings have significance in the abstract relationship of their colors as much as in their subject matter. *Day on Which* applies that lesson to the art of the stage. Williams, who wrote an essay about Hofmann in 1948, was friendly with several of the artist's students and models in Provincetown and New York. Incidentally, the implication that the artist is working nude in the first scene is taken from a habit of Hofmann's, not Pollock's.

On the Ginza the woman is, as she says, wearing a cool-colored suit. While she sips her tea, a second stagehand enters and stands beside the table with a large paper poppy, one last red image—a connection of the painter's wounds, his mouth, and his art.

Although the main character has died, the play goes on past its obvious climax. This is non-Western dramatic structure, and Williams subtitled his text "An Occidental Noh Play." Noh is a fourteenth-century Japanese theater form combining dance, music, storytelling, and enactment. *Day* uses a similar combination on stage. There is another reason for the subtitle: the purpose of Noh. Simply put, if Western comedy intends to make audiences laugh, and Western tragedy intends to make audiences cry, the intent of Noh is to make audiences feel *yugen*—"still beauty." Williams achieves this effect with color.

The scene shifts again, and the color sequence progresses. A Japanese narrator, in a role called The Oriental, addresses the audience. He opens up the back wall in the stage right space to reveal "a morning sky, a white cloud drifting across it." After all that red, which fatigues the eye, the blue is welcome and restful. The appearance of the pure morning sky—and the reflex effect on the audience's eyes—is the *yugen* of the piece: still beauty on stage and in the audience.

The woman reenters the red-splashed studio to mourn the painter's crumpled body. By the conclusion of *Day on Which* the interplay of red with a contrasting cool color parallels the contrast of a corpse with the eternal sky, and the contrast of the public expression of emotion with private contemplation.

The last idea is reinforced by the position of the actors' bodies. The mourning woman, aware she is to face an audience, adjusts her makeup in a mirror. The Japanese stagehand contemplates the sky with his back turned to the public.

The play was not produced during Williams lifetime. Its vision of self-damnation led to Williams next major play, *The Night of the Iguana*, where damnation is averted by the miracle of redemptive love. In the film adaptation of *Iguana*, the two stagehands from *Day on Which* were translated into the pair of cabana boys shadowing Ava Gardner; the artist's bloody footsteps were given to Richard Burton. Williams rewrote the story of his Jackson Pollock-like painter for *In the Bar of a Tokyo Hotel*, yet *Day on Which* shares not a single line with *Tokyo Hotel*—and more importantly there is no painting on stage and no suicide in *Tokyo Hotel*. Although Williams employed color in later plays, there is nothing so color-dependent as *The Day on Which a Man Dies*, where subject matter and form of expression fuse. The manuscript, cataloged as "finished" in Williams handwriting, went unnoticed in a California library until 1991. It was first performed in Chicago in February 2008 and published later that spring. In 2009 the production was revived in Chicago, then toured to the places where this striking work's conception began: to East Hampton where it was produced in conjunction with the Pollock Krasner House & Study Center, then up to Provincetown to the main gallery of the Provincetown Art Association and Museum. In September 2015, *The Day on Which a Man Dies* played in repertory with *The Milk Train Doesn't Stop Here Anymore*, both texts performed by the same actors from Abrahamse-Meyer Productions of Cape Town, South Africa.

The Milk Train Doesn't Stop Here Anymore: Look at What We Got Away With

The Milk Train Doesn't Stop Here Anymore, Jennifer Steyn as Flora Goforth, directed by Fred Abrahamse, Artscape and Abrahamse-Meyer Productions, Cape Town, South Africa. TW Fest 2013. Photo Josh Andrus.

When *The Milk Train Doesn't Stop Here Anymore* opened on Broadway in 1963 it was reviled. Hated. Despised. You have to ask yourself, what got them so angry, those critics? What was it about the show that they finally had had enough of Tennessee Williams? Was it that he didn't engage in the Civil Rights movement, which was raging still in Mississippi that year? And Mississippi is where Williams was born; he might have said something. That he didn't reveal, yet, his own sexuality? Frank Merlo, his lover of fourteen years was dying and he might have made a play about that. Instead Williams put an old horny woman on stage, someone who wasn't afraid of calling herself a monster, who had flags with griffins made to wave as an emblem of her monstrousness for all to see. Is that what did it? Were

they provoked by the title that was, to say the least, obscure and confusing? Was it the pair of droll Japanese stagehands Williams had been farming out in plays since he decided to shelve *The Day on Which a Man Dies*, his Noh drama parable of Jackson Pollock's self-destruction, and sent the boys off to Puerto Vallarta to service Flora's kissing cousin Maxine in *Night of the Iguana*? In *Milk Train*, which takes place in Italy, there's no excuse to have one Japanese stagehand, much less two. That's a distracting irritation, thinking about that, while waiting for…what?

What were they waiting for, those Broadway critics, what were they listening for, that they didn't fall for the charms of Flora Goforth's voice—delicate, haughty, hushed, brazen—resounding down the mountains to the world's oldest sea as she dictates her lurid memoirs over a loudspeaker? Were the critics so busy trying to unravel or dismiss Williams' easy obvious symbolism that they missed the significance of Williams writing a play in which the appetite for love transcends the limitations of the body? You know what I think it is that made them hate the play? It's that there isn't anyone in it who is nice. Witty, yes. Nice, no. Perhaps that's it: Flora is great, as great as Lear, and as likable as Lear; neither Lear nor Flora are as likable as Mr. and Mrs. Santa Claus at the Mall of America. Nor does Flora earn compassion as a miserable martyr. No, Flora's no martyr; she's self-satisfied and at the same time always needy. The Angel of Death has come to call on her in the person of a blonde young poet and she wants to fuck him. Could that have been it? I think, maybe so, I think that's what left the critics not cold but hot with anger, that Williams at this point in his life, while his lover was coughing to death, at the time when Medgar Evers was shot dead, had nothing more important to offer than a confession: that, as far as he could see, there was nothing to be done in this world of humiliations to gain dignity, nothing. What we have to counter death is lust as much as love, and lust isn't dignified, no, not at all—and if it's inevitable that death will pull the rings off our fingers and our soul out of our flesh, then let's, while we can, not even try to remain dignified, but marvel at what we've gotten away with so far before we expire. Let's marvel at what won't last, can't last—our lives—marvel, while we can, that the Angel of Death standing before the sea where he found his vocation, according to Williams, will recognize our annihilation by saying along with the waves *Boom*, like a Hindu's mantra, or a Zen master's koan, *Boom*. Before we die we can say *Boom* too and, like Flora Goforth, marvel that even if our lives came to nothing, look at what we got away with: pleasure while it lasted, the pleasure of seeing, loving, writing—Williams would have had to include writing, it gave him so much pleasure. Think of Flora's pleasures: dressing up, stripping, lying, telling the truth, sometimes. *Boom.*

Kingdom of Earth: From Cape Town to Cape Cod and Back

From Cape Town, South Africa, to the tip of Cape Cod, Massachusetts, and back—and back again—the award-winning staging of Tennessee Williams' often overlooked, late play *Kingdom of Earth* from Abrahamse-Meyer Productions is a not to be overlooked example of what the Tennessee Williams Festival in Provincetown means and does to act on its mission, to roll out Tennessee Williams' work into the world.

In late September 2012, the meeting hall of the musty Provincetown VFW on Highway 6 opened to the beat of Sam Chatmon's haunting Mississippi Delta blues song "I Have to Paint my Face":

Say God made us all
He made some at night

Kingdom of Earth, *Abrahamse Meyer Productions, Cape Town, South Africa. Marcel Meyer, as Chicken, directed by Fred Abrahamse. TW Fest 2012. Photo Josh Andrus.*

> That's why he didn't take time
> To make us all white

The sight of Marcel Meyer at ease in a hyper-masculine pose, stripped to the waist, pouring water on himself, readies the audience to pay close attention to the entrance of Anthea Thompson in hot pink, gingham Capri pants stretched over ample assets. She's playing Myrtle, an ex-stripper prattling in a spot-on country-fried accent, mysteriously acquired 8,700 miles from the Mississippi Delta, where the play is set. Myrtle got married the day before to neurasthenic Lot, played with albino blonde perfection by Nicholas Dallas. Lot aims to have Myrtle set up home on his family farm, though he didn't bother to tell his new wife about his half-brother named Chicken, who lives on the place. That's Meyer as Chicken, feral, glistening wet, listening to their arrival.

A Boston-based critic described what it was like to be in the audience:

> As directed by Fred Abrahamse, the play grabbed hold of your throat and slowly, purposefully, squeezed your breath away….The effect was riveting. (Robert Israel, *Edge Magazine*)

The South African cast flew into Boston two days before their festival premiere, thanks to last-minute intercession to get the proper visas from America's Vice Consul in Cape Town, Collier F. Graham, who coincidentally hails from Clarksdale, Mississippi, where Tennessee Williams spent his boyhood. Clarksdale is the next town over from where *Kingdom of Earth* takes place. In a fortuitous Washington meeting between Robert Gips, US ambassador to South Africa, and Ebrahim Rasool, South African ambassador to the United States, the two diplomats discussed the hope that South African theater artists would bring a new point of view to a version of a play better known, and known to be bad, as *The Seven Descents of Myrtle*.

Under that ungainly title, the play opened on Broadway the day after Williams' birthday in 1968 and ran for twenty-nine performances. The critics were baffled:

> There is no rational explanation of *The Seven Descents of Myrtle* except that Tennessee Williams is burlesquing himself, if that is rational. Williams' exercises in southern degradation have sometimes illuminated the human condition, but this one is narrow, obsessively petty, and essentially ludicrous. (Edwin Newman, NBC News)

Forty-four years later, the South African production brought a different perspective, in particular a sensitivity to the issues of race that underscore the play, something unnoticed in 1968, so distracted were Americans by the playwright's unapologetic homosexuality. What was called burlesque—Williams' reconfiguration of his earlier themes under the light of his later experience—is now recognized as the widening of his vision as a creative artist. Knowing the Festival's enthusiasm for presenting adventurous work written by Williams, Tom Erhardt, the London-based theater agent from Casarotto Ramsay who represented the Tennessee Williams estate, suggested that the Abrahamse-Meyer production premiere in Provincetown.

Critical theory aside, visceral enjoyment of the performances in Provincetown was undeniable. The run sold out. Home in Cape Town, South Africa, where it played next, the production was acclaimed. "The cast are, without exception, absolutely outstanding," said the *Cape Times*, commending the "terrible beauty" of the acting and pointing out that "the play is ultimately one of hope. It is a resounding affirmation of the power of love." The production was nominated for three Fleur du Cap Awards (the Cape Town equivalent of the Tony). Anthea Thompson was nominated for best actress, Charl-Johan Lingenfelder for original score, and Fred Abrahamse won for the best set design.

The further resonance of the production is impressive. Brenda Caradine, the executive director of the Columbus, Mississippi, Tennessee Williams Tribute, had been coming to Provincetown for each of the previous eight years of the Tennessee Williams Festival. She was so moved by *Kingdom of Earth* that she had her own production of it staged in Columbus—the small town where Williams was born. Echoing the Provincetown VFW, an old drugstore on the historic downtown Main Street of Columbus was converted into an intimate theater. M. J. Etua directed, with Alex Orsak as Lot, Cherri Golden as Myrtle. A reviewer in Columbus extolled David Trotter in the role of Chicken:

> [He] both dazzled and disturbed the audience.
>
> The honesty that defined the complexity of a man who is tormented by his own existence was felt throughout his entire performance. The subtleties of anger, hate, madness and shame permeated his performance. No emotions were left unaddressed. (Joseph St. John, *This Is Real Media*)

Mississippi social mores are not Provincetown's. The play was controversial in Columbus, its impoliteness "disappointing," and emails circulated protesting Williams' "objectionable language." And this, too, the reviewer in Columbus took on:

> Tennessee Williams was a man before his time…a true philosopher of the human condition. He did not mince his words as he dealt with the complex issues of race, sex, passion, heterosexuality, homosexuality and the Eros of humanity…Some people may not like what Tennessee Williams had to say and that is their loss. Williams accomplished what all

writers want to be: an artist who says, writes and does whatever he wants. In the end, he was the master of his own art.

Joe Paprzycki, the artistic director of the South Camden Theatre Company in New Jersey, also comes to the Tennessee Williams Festival in Provincetown every year. His productions of Williams' plays *Suddenly Last Summer* and *The Night of the Iguana* have brought his company great reviews. A production of *Kingdom of Earth*, directed by Connie Norwood, opened the 2013 season in Camden, starting in October. Paprzycki explained: "I knew about the play before, and had probably read it, maybe even more than once, but seeing it was something else. Seeing the South African production at the Festival inspired me to produce it."

The genesis of these inspired connections began in 2006, when a small group of people gathered in Boston to draw up a mission statement for the Provincetown Tennessee Williams Theater Festival. The agreed-on goals: to celebrate Williams' work and connection to Provincetown, but also to send the spirit—"searching spirit," was suggested—rolling forward out of the Cape and back. That is what has happened to *Kingdom of Earth*. The original South African company returned to the 2013 Provincetown Festival and played to sold-out houses.

Kingdom of Earth, *Abrahamse Meyer Productions, Cape Town, South Africa. Nicholas Dallas as Lot, directed by Fred Abrahamse, TW Fest 2012. Photo Josh Andrus.*

The Two-Character Play and Matisse

In the winter of 2012, a few months before Tennessee Williams' *The Two-Character Play* began a run in Manhattan, there was a show at the Metropolitan Museum of Art about Matisse becoming Matisse. Forty-nine paintings were shown for purposes of comparison. With Tennessee Williams and his repurposing of realism in mind, I stopped to stare at a pair of paintings. On the canvas I suppose was painted first, Matisse depicted the corner of a room with a view—of Nice I think. There's curved iron grille work below a window, two goldfish hang in a glass bucket, a leggy houseplant curves up out of a little terracotta pot, there's a plain table, a pillowed couch, an empty bowl, all of these painted as if in the diffused blue of twilight, arranged as conventionally as they would be in a photograph.

The other painting of the pair contains the same things arranged in a different composition: the iron curves float in the air behind and below the fish, which still hang in the glass bucket. The plant droops from behind the bucket. We don't see the little

The Glass Menagerie, *Actors Theater of Alabama, Birmingham, Alabama, Amanda Maddox as Laura, directed by Will York. TW Fest 2012. Photo by Josh Andrus.*

terracotta pot, an orange on the table replaces it, rhyming the color of the fish. The couch and the pillows are flattened to colored trapezoids as are the walls and the floor. There is no view, there is no room. We're looking at a point of view.

And that's how Matisse became Matisse, by mastering the elements of realistic composition and then recombining them into something essential, thereby creating a painting that was frankly a painting—and its subject matter is as much painting as it is any nice or Nice view.

Tennessee Williams is doing the same with *The Two-Character Play*: the conspiratorial relationship of brother and sister he'd written about in *The Glass Menagerie*—and lived all his life—is reconfigured past realism or reality to become a play about a play.

Why? Because, three decades after *Glass Menagerie* opened in Chicago, Tennessee Williams had thirty more years to think about his subject matter, and he knew more, and he felt more—and differently—about his subject matter. Her name, Rose, crops up in nearly every Williams' play like the Ninas in a Hirschfeld, but in this play once only, when the playwright-brother tells his sister:

I know what to do.

And she replies:

Oh, do you? What is it? To sit there staring all day at a threadbare rose in a carpet until it withers?

Three decades after *The Glass Menagerie* opened on Broadway, the playwright had time enough to reflect upon his ability to turn memories into stage business: enjoying international fame, making a good living by entertaining strangers with the intimacies of his family, while Rose was lobotomized and kept apart from the world in a series of institutions. In *The Two-Character Play* a brother has written a play for himself and his sister to perform, and the playwright's sister has feelings about being cast in her brother's play, which she's been touring around the world for, well, probably as long as *The Glass Menagerie* has been tinkling away on stages throughout the world.

The same elements that construct the illusion of the *Menagerie* living-room recombine in *The Two-Character Play*'s stagy setting: the soap bubble of happy memories, self-crippling shyness, the braggadocio of a born story-teller, Southern gentility facing the shame of owing money at the Jewish Deli—Garfinkel's in *Menagerie*, Grossman's in *Two-Character*.

The Two-Character Play is a play about the making and makers of artifice, fueled by the same realities that fuel the *Glass Menagerie*: the realities of pride and regret, love and disappointment, and—as in all of Williams' plays—the reality that words can be incantations of light against the dark.

By removing the responsibility of creating a stage illusion from his words, in *The Two-Character Play* Williams frees his play from portraiture and plotline as decisively as Matisse pulls our eyes out of the corner of a room to look instead at the center of an essence. In *The Two-Character Play* we look and listen to the essence of Williams' writing, as the playwright-brother says to his sister while the stage lights dim:

If we can imagine summer, we can imagine more light.

Which brings the sister to a question:

If we're lost in the play?

In some editions of the text her words end with period, so it's not a question but the sister's statement. In all editions there's the same response.

Yes, completely lost in *The Two-Character Play*.

Glass Guignol, a workshop of a fantasia on The Two-Character Play *directed by Lee Breuer. Mabou Mines, New York. Maude Mitchell, as Rose manifested through Clare of* The Two-Character Play, Laura *and Amanda of* The Glass Menagerie, Nance *of* A Cavalier for My Lady, *and Catharine Holly of* Suddenly Last Summer. TW Fest 2011. Photo by Josh Andrus.

Nineteen Eighty: Surviving Beyond What is Acceptable

David Landon as Mister Paradise, directed by David Kaplan, The Hotel Plays *in New Orleans, 2014. Detail of a photo by Ride Hamilton.*

Lateness is the idea of surviving beyond what is acceptable and normal.
—Theodor Adorno (rephrased by Edward Said)

By 1980 Tennessee Williams had experienced eighteen years of rejection since the last year of his heyday, when *The Night of the Iguana* opened on Broadway in 1961. It was time enough to reconsider the purposes of his work and its relationship to the expectations of critics and crowds. He had, it has been said, lived past his time. Even so, he continued to write despite illness, some of it self-induced: the effects of long term—and continuing—drug and alcohol abuse. The year began for Williams in Key West. On New Year's Eve he went out for a pizza with a group of friends, including the actor Paul Lynde. His agent, Mitch Douglas, led the group in singing "Auld Lang Syne." Later that month his play *Will Mr. Merriwether Return from Memphis?* premiered at the opening

of the Tennessee Williams Performing Arts Center in Key West. The text, written in 1969, includes a séance where heroes of the playwright—Vincent van Gogh, Rimbaud, Hart Crane—return from death to visit people who don't know who they are (an arch reference to Williams' own condition). It had been eighteen years since he'd had a hit.

In 1980, he flew off so frequently from Key West to New York, New Orleans, Chicago, London, Sicily, and British Columbia that he seemed to have turned into that fantastical thing he had once described in *Orpheus Descending*: a bird who sleeps on the wind.

As the months passed, Williams worked on and completed two full-length plays: *Clothes for a Summer Hotel*, a meditation on the lives of Scott and Zelda Fitzgerald, and *The Notebooks of Trigorin*, an interpretation of Chekhov's *The Seagull*. At the same time he drafted several short plays, finishing at least four of them: the grotesquely funny *This Is Peaceable Kingdom* or *Good Luck God*, which is set during a strike of hospital workers in New York City; *Some Problems for the Moose Lodge*, a dark family comedy set in Mississippi and performed in Chicago that year; *Steps Must be Gentle*, an elegiac homage to the poet Hart Crane; *The Traveling Companion*, a perceptive self-analysis; and *The Chalky White Substance*, an apocalyptic fantasy set in the distant future, perhaps partly inspired by the eruption of Mount Saint Helen's on May 18, 1980.

On March 26, 1980, Williams' sixty-ninth birthday, *Clothes for a Summer Hotel* opened on Broadway. Walter Kerr, who in 1952, had called *Camino Real,* "the worst play by the best playwright" once again yearned for the familiar Williams and wrote: "the most dismaying thing about Tennessee Williams's pursuit of the ghosts of Scott and Zelda Fitzgerald, 'Clothes for a Summer Hotel,' is the fact that Mr. Williams' personal voice is nowhere to be heard in it." The production closed soon after, Williams' last Broadway play during his lifetime. During rehearsals Williams would run downtown to catch performances on the Bowery of the unruly *Kirche, Küche, und Kinder*, subtitled *An Outrage for the Stage*.

Williams' mother died June 1 at the age of ninety-five. The playwright was on Long Island, New York the night the call came to tell him so, but waited until morning to respond. A week later, Williams was in Washington, D.C. receiving the Medal of Freedom. By mid-June he was in London, en route to Sicily with the painter Henry Faulkner, a friend from Key West. In Sicily the friends had a falling out, and Williams returned to the States.

By August 1980, Williams was back in Key West, working on some new one-act plays, *The Traveling Companion* and *Chalky White Substance*. In October 1980, he was invited to Vancouver as writer-in-residence while a production of a revised The *Red Devil Battery Sign*, originally written in 1975, was rehearsed and performed. Its success was a vindication of the text, scorned in

Boston for its "incoherence." On November 8 Williams was in Chicago for the Goodman Theater's opening of *Tennessee Laughs*. The Goodman invited him to expand *Some Problems for the Moose Lodge* to full-length.

Eight new plays in one year. Two successful revivals. A Broadway failure. Even so, Williams' future, despite visions of apocalyptic doom, was promising.

In the next year, 1981, Williams' hopes were dashed again and again. A major autobiographical play, *Something Cloudy, Something Clear* opened New York at the Cocteau Repertory Theatre, but was met with disappointed and unflattering reviews. The rewrite of *Moose Lodge*, now a full-length play titled *A House Not Meant to Stand*, opened in Chicago to mixed notices. His long-time agent and advocate Audrey Wood fell into an irreversible coma. He had a falling out with his current agent. Henry Faulkner and another long-term friend, Oliver Evans, died that fall. In December, Lincoln Center in New York cancelled a gala to celebrate his 70th birthday: not enough tickets had been sold.

Nineteen eighty-two was also difficult; a highlight was the valedictory retrospective of his work produced that summer at the Williamstown Theater Festival along with a workshop production of a new play: *Gideon's Point*. Williams was actively involved in choosing the retrospective material and arranging it.

In September, however, he left home, his cat and dog both ran off, and he gave away his typewriter to a stranger he met in the Florida Keys.

Even so Williams remained open to new projects. In the spring of 1982, the Goodman Theatre in Chicago mounted a new version of *A House Not Meant to Stand*, in the summer a young film director had a plan to adapt some short stories. Yet friends noticed a falling away in New York. Early in 1983 he was depressed about the Lincoln Center event, over a year after it happened. His companion at the time says he had stopped writing every morning—surely a sign of change. His last play, completed late that January, was titled *The One Exception*, and seemed to imagine what would happen to his sister Rose after he himself had gone. Less than a month later, Williams passed away February 25, 1983, one month shy of his 72nd birthday.

The best I could say for myself is that I worked like hell.
(Tennessee Williams, *Notebooks*, 1979)

Williams' open enjoyment of sex, bitter humor, shameless melodrama, grotesquerie, cruelty, and paranoia—and his flaunting of conventional taste and logic—mostly laid low, but never lay fallow. The fullness of his imagining led to plays that were neither written for immediate publication or performance, but for himself and perhaps (if we want to flatter ourselves) with hopes that in the future an audience might appreciate what he was writing: read it, stage it, publish it.

Let us conclude at least this: that there is no conclusion to Williams' reputation, it unfolds.

Provincetown Tennessee Williams Theater Festival Programing 2006–2015

2006 Tennessee Williams in Provincetown

By Tennessee Williams

27 Wagons Full of Cotton

The Eccentricities of a Nightingale (scenes in Cantonese)

The Glass Menagerie

The Parade or *Approaching the End of a Summer* (world premiere)

The Unsatisfactory Supper

This Property is Condemned

Adapted from Williams

A Streetcar Named Desire choreographed by Valerie Bettis (ballet)

A Streetcar Named Desire screenplay by Tennessee Williams and Oscar Saul (1951 film)

A Streetcar Named Desire composed by Andre Previn (scenes from the opera)

Baby Doll by Tennessee Williams (film)

The Fugitive Kind, screenplay by Meade Roberts with Tennessee Williams (film)

The Roman Spring of Mrs. Stone, screenplay by Gavin Lambert and Jan Read (film)

The Road to Paradise by Carson Efird (dance and poetry)

The Strange, the Crazed, the Queer by David Landon (music and poetry)

The Yellow Bird, screenplay by Faye Dunaway (film)

Inspired by Williams

The Foggy Foggy Dew by Wendy Kesselman (staged reading)

The Plexiglas Menagerie by Ryan Landry (staged reading)

Williams in Short Shorts (one-act plays from the New Provincetown Players)

2007 The Late Late Show

By Tennessee Williams

Camino Real

I Can't Imagine Tomorrow

Sunburst (world premiere)

The Chalky White Substance

The Demolition Downtown

The Gnädiges Fräulein

The Municipal Abattoir

The One Exception

The Parade or Approaching the End of a Summer

The Pronoun "I" (world premiere)

The Traveling Companion

Adapted from Williams

Everybody Expects Me to Write Another Streetcar by Jeremy Lawrence

Noir et Blanc by Claire Devers (film)

The Drift by John Aes-Nihil (film)

The Migrants by Lanford Wilson (film)

The Road to Paradise by Carson Efird (dance and poetry)

The Roman Spring of Mrs. Stone, screenplay by Gavin Lambert and Jan Read (1961 film)

The Roman Spring of Mrs. Stone, screenplay by Martin Sherman (2003 TV film)

The Notebook of Trigorin adapted by Katherine Mendeloff

The Strange, the Crazed, the Queer by David Landon (music and poetry)

SUMMER? by John Aes-Nihil (film)

Inspired by Williams

Tennessee Rocks: Rick Knudsen, Clyde Shelby, and John Thomas (music)

The Foggy Foggy Dew by Wendy Kesselman

The Ghost Plays (one-act plays from the New Provincetown Players)

The Plexiglas Menagerie by Ryan Landry

Related Plays by Other Authors

Come and Go by Samuel Beckett

The Stronger by August Strindberg

Special Presentations

Coffee with John Guare

Ethel Elkovsky Recites with Mia Phoebus

Homage to Valeska Gert with Susanne Foellmer

I am the Moon and You are the Man on Me with Julie Atlas Muz and Tigger! Ferguson

"Tennessee Williams is never apolitical" with Amiri Baraka

"Tennessee Williams: Theater in Process" with Annette Cardona

2008 The Healing Power of Love

By Tennessee Williams

Adam and Eve on a Ferry

Camino Real

Green Eyes (world premiere)

The Dog Enchanted by the Divine View (world premiere)

The Eccentricities of a Nightingale (scenes)

Adapted from Williams

Lorita! adapted from "Happy August the Tenth" by Paula Frasz (dance)

Summer and Smoke composed by Lee Hoiby (opera)

Inspired by Williams

Rancho Pancho by Gregg Barrios

Young Love (one-act plays from the New Provincetown Players)

Special Presentations

Coffee with Eli Wallach and Anne Jackson

Olympia Dukakis, "From *Streetcar* to *Milk Train*"

Tennessee in Foreign Tongues (in Portuguese, Russian, Malayalam, Cantonese, French) (video)

2009 The Fight for Life

By Tennessee Williams

A Streetcar Named Desire

Hello from Bertha

Mister Paradise

Talk To Me Like the Rain and Let Me Listen…

Thank You, Kind Spirit

The Case of the Crushed Petunias

The Enemy: Time (world premiere)

The Day on Which a Man Dies

The Lady of Larkspur Lotion

The Last of My Solid Gold Watches

The Pink Bedroom

The Remarkable Rooming-House of Mme. Le Monde (world premiere)

The Strangest Kind of Romance

Adapted from Williams

Ghosts from a Summer Hotel adapted by David Kaplan

Val's Story by Fran Weinberg

Inspired by Williams

21 Gun Salute by Jay Critchley (performance art)

Wartime in P'Town by CTEK (street theater)

Related plays by other authors

Miss Julie by August Strindberg (in Norwegian)

Special Presentation

Coffee With Lanford Wilson

2010 Under the Influence

By Tennessee Williams

27 Wagons Full of Cotton

American Gothic (world premiere)

Escape

Orpheus Descending

Suddenly Last Summer (staged reading)

Summer at the Lake

Inspired by Williams

Bent to the Flame by Doug Tompos

Laughing In the Dark with Tennessee compiled by John DiLeo (film)

Orpheus in the Galleries (collage, sculpture, assemblage, painting)

The Escapes by Paula Frasz (dance)

The Jazz Funeral of Stella Brooks by Terry Abrahamson (music)

Related plays by other authors

Diff'rent by Eugene O'Neill

Special Presentation

Coffee With William Jay Smith

2011 Double Exposures

By Tennessee Williams

Now the Cats with Jewelled Claws

Once in a Lifetime (world premiere)

Orpheus Descending

Something Cloudy, Something Clear

The Parade or *Approaching the End of a Summer*

The Two-Character Play

Adapted from Williams

Dirty Shorts: "The Killer Chicken and the Closet Queen" & "Miss Coynte of Greene" (staged reading)

Williams Wrote Here by Jeremy Lawrence

Inspired by Williams

Alma by Rita Calçada Bastos (performance art)

South Pathetic by Jim David

Special Presentation

"Glass Guignol" A Master Class with Lee Breuer

2012 Tennessee Williams and Music

By Tennessee Williams

Auto-da-Fé

I Never Get Dressed Till After Dark on Sundays

Kingdom of Earth

Ten Blocks on the Camino Real

The Glass Menagerie

This Property Is Condemned (in Italian)

Portrait of a Madonna (in Italian)

The Unsatisfactory Supper (in Italian)

The Dark Room (in Italian)

Adapted from Williams

Gift of an Orange by Charlene A. Donaghy
Autumn Song by George Maurer
The South is Everywhere by Herb Krill (video)
The Tennessee Williams Songbook by David Kaplan

Special Presentations

Coffee with Mitch Douglass
Magnolia Jam with Terry "Harmonica" Bean

2013 Tennessee Williams and Women

By Tennessee Williams

At Liberty
Cairo, Shanghai, Bombay!
Cat On A Hot Tin Roof
Curtains for the Gentleman (world premiere)
The Mutilated
Kingdom of Earth
The Milk Train Doesn't Stop Here Anymore

Inspired by Williams

The Chorus Girls by Paula Frasz (dance)

Related plays by other authors

Pink Melon Joy by Gertrude Stein
In the Summer House by Jane Bowles

Special Presentations

"A Neo-Benshi Streetcar, Miss Lulu Bett, and Rebel Without a Cause" with Roxi Power
Mississippi Juke Joint with Eden Brent

2014 Circle of Friends

By Tennessee Williams

A Lovely Sunday for Creve Coeur
Period of Adjustment
Vieux Carré

Adapted from Williams

I Wish You'd Keep Still choreographed by Carson Efird (dance)

Related plays by other authors

The Boy in the Basement, *The Killing*, *The Love Death*, and *The Tiny Closet* by William Inge
The Lady Aoi by Yukio Mishima
The Member of the Wedding by Carson McCullers (staged reading)

Special Presentations

Beatnik Jam with Jeremy Lawrence and Joseph Merlo III

John Lahr: Tennessee Williams and His friends

2015 Tennessee Williams in Provincetown, 2006–2015

By Tennessee Williams

Aimez-Vouz Ionesco? (world premiere)

Suddenly Last Summer

The Day on Which a Man Dies

The Milk Train Doesn't Stop Here Any More

The Parade or *Approaching the End of a Summer*

The Remarkable Rooming-House of Mme Le Monde

Adapted from Williams

Canciónes de Tennessee Williams by David Kaplan (music)

More Stars than there are in Heaven by John Guare (staged reading)

Road to Paradise choreographed by Carson Efird (dance and poetry)

Tenn at Town Hall adapted by Jef Hall-Flavin (staged reading)

The Liberation of Colette Simple by Vincent Guibert (music)

Detail of a charcoal drawing by Bill Evaul, 2012. Inspired by Auto-da-Fé *a one-act play by Tennessee Williams.*

www.ingramcontent.com/pod-product-compliance
Lightning Source LLC
Chambersburg PA
CBHW040903020526
44114CB00037B/42